THE POWER DRESSERS

THE POWER DRESSERS

A WOMEN'S GUIDE TO PROFESSIONAL STYLE

MICHELE GRANT

Copyright © 2023 Michele Grant.

All rights reserved.

Published by Thales Publishing, USA

The Power Dressers™: A Women's Guide to Professional Style by Michele Grant

ISBN 978-0-9896668-5-5 (hardcover)
ISBN 978-0-9896668-0-0 (paperback)
ISBN 978-0-9896668-2-4 (eBook)

Printed in the United States of America

Cover design by Xavier Comas de la Paz, photo credit Michael Benabib
Interior design by Morgane Leoni
Interior photo credits Michael Benabib, Joseph Stella Studio,
Roger Archer, and Michele Grant

Cover and Interior Copyright © 2024 Michele Grant

Bulk discounts available. For details visit: www.powerdressers.com

No part of this publication may be reproduced, distributed, stored in a retrieval system, or transmitted in whole or in part, in any form or by any means, including electronic, mechanical, photocopying, recording, or otherwise, without the prior written permission of the author, Michele Grant. except in the case of brief quotations embodied in critical reviews and certain other noncommercial uses permitted by copyright law.

The content within this book, including but not limited to the text, graphics, images, and other material, is the original work and property of the author, Michele Grant, and is protected by copyright and other intellectual property laws. The information provided is for the reader's personal, non-commercial use only and may not be used for any commercial purpose or redistributed in any form without the author's explicit permission.

The author and publisher are not responsible for websites (or their content) that are not owned by the publisher or author.

To my loving and endlessly reassuring husband, Lawrence,
my incredible children, Gabriele and Isaiah,
and my beloved brother, Nigel –
Thank you for believing in me every step of the way.
Your love and support were blessings along this creative journey.

Above all, I thank God for the strength and perseverance to see this dream fulfilled,
and for the enduring legacy of my mother, Dr. Ava.

"I can do all things through Christ who strengthens me."
- Philippians 4:13

Table of Contents

introduction
Unlocking Your Inner Power Dresser
8

chapter 1
Unleashing the Transformative Power of Professional Style
12

chapter 2
Dressing for Your Body Type: The Power Dresser's Approach
32

chapter 3
Embracing the Psychology and Power of Color in Professional Style
52

chapter 4
Building a Professional Wardrobe with Sustainability and Style in Mind
80

chapter 5

Navigating Professional Dress Codes
102

chapter 6

Learning the Nonverbal and Cultural Languages of Professional Attire
134

chapter 7

Enhancing Your Style with Accessories, Footwear, and Grooming
156

chapter 8

Staying Fashion-Forward in Your Professional Life
180

the grand finale

From Style Novices to Power Dressers
200

introduction

UNLOCKING YOUR INNER POWER DRESSER

Have you ever entered a room and immediately felt the energy shift in your favor? This is usually because people noticed your physical appearance, confidence, and power. The essence of a Power Dresser is a woman who skillfully blends professional style with personal energy, thus captivating attention and earning respect in any environment.

In my two decades as a successful female professional in the corporate world, I've encountered my fair share of challenges as well as celebrating hard-earned victories. But one constant factor that has played an indispensable role in my success has been my ability to dress for the part. I've seen first-hand how dressing in a way that projects authority and confidence can open doors, win over clients, unlock opportunities, forge connections, and propel my career forward.

My journey began as a fresh graduate entering the corporate world, eager to make my mark but still trying to figure out how to dress for success. I quickly realized that my wardrobe needed development, but I did not know where to begin. I spent hours researching, shopping, and experimenting with various styles, until I found the best formula for me – building a collection of timeless classics and statement pieces, and honing a keen eye for detail.

As I navigated my career path, I began understanding the power of professional dressing. It wasn't just about looking good; it was about feeling good, too. My confidence and stature blossomed as my wardrobe mirrored my inner strength, and I could see its impact on my career trajectory. Notably, colleagues and clients started perceiving me differently, recognizing my assertive presence well before any verbal exchange occurred between us.

Your professional style is also a form of nonverbal communication. It sends a message to those around you, about who you are and what you represent. Your dress, body language, and presentation contribute to your professional image. Creating a consistent message to support career aspirations involves focusing on nonverbal cues and how you present yourself in any setting.

The choice of your clothing holds great power. This book is a guide to dressing impeccably, making a lasting impression, and becoming the best version of yourself. You can become an unstoppable Power Dresser by applying the lessons I've learned, and this book's advice. Take this transformative journey and watch your career soar.

In the words of the legendary costume designer Edith Head, "Dress shabbily and they notice the dress. Dress impeccably and they notice the woman."

Embarking on your journey to becoming a Power Dresser involves self-reflection, learning, and growth. As you work through the various elements of professional style, you'll understand its undeniable impact on your career trajectory and the impression you are making on others.

As explored in a 2011 Harvard Business Review article by Stone, people who dress professionally are perceived as more competent, trustworthy, and intelligent. This perception can directly affect your career path and opportunities for advancement. Furthermore, dressing professionally helps create a strong and lasting first impression, which can improve your performance in job interviews, promotion reviews, and networking situations.

This underscores the importance of cultivating a professional aesthetic that aligns with your brand and career goals. By dressing with intention and understanding the power of your clothing choices, you can effectively project an image of authority and competence that other people will respond to with positivity.

In the following chapters, you'll be introduced to practical tips and strategies to help you make informed decisions about your wardrobe — a wardrobe that communicates your unique qualities and strengths. You will be encouraged to reflect on your current wardrobe, identify areas for improvement, and gradually make changes that align with your aspirations. When you incorporate the lessons learned from my journey and the insights gained from my research and practice, you will be well on your way to embodying the Power Dresser you were meant to be.

The key to this process is not to be swayed by the transient allure of fashion or the sheen of luxury brands; it's about finding that inner resonance with your authentic self and allowing it to radiate through every ensemble you choose. The journey may be challenging, but the rewards will be worth the effort. So, are you ready to unlock your inner Power Dresser? Are you prepared to embark on this journey and discover the true impact of professional dressing on your career and personal growth?

The time is now, the power is yours to grasp, and the potential for success is limitless.

Let's begin.

UNLEASHING THE TRANSFORMATIVE POWER OF PROFESSIONAL STYLE

chapter 1

A single glance across the room was all it took for me to realize that I was in an unfamiliar situation. As a young professional, I was attending my first crucial meeting, and I realized my attire conveyed my inexperience. The women in the conference room looked confident and authoritative, while my passé ensemble made me feel anything but empowered. That moment was the catalyst for my transformation, my first step to becoming a Power Dresser.

In this chapter, you will learn:

- **The essence of professional style**
- **The benefits of professional style for confidence, credibility, and respect**
- **The impact of attire on first impressions**
- **How your professional image affects your career**
- **The path to constructing a professional wardrobe**

The Essence of Professional Style

One typical weekday morning, I was in the middle of preparing for a client meeting. With my nerves slightly on edge, I knew that my choice of attire would be a critical factor in setting the tone for the meeting and building credibility with the client. Standing in front of my closet, I considered my options carefully, knowing that my professional style would speak volumes about my capabilities, even before I uttered a single word.

Professional style is not merely about dressing in a suit or donning a crisp white shirt. It's an intricate blend of personal expression, power, and credibility. It's about understanding the nuances of color, fit, and texture and using them to create an outfit that exudes confidence and authority. It's about owning your presence and making a memorable statement of trustworthiness and competence to those around you.

Let's take a minute to walk through the critical elements of professional style:

1. **FIT:**
   How your clothes fit your body is vital to creating a polished and sophisticated appearance. Ill-fitting garments can detract from your overall look, so invest in well-tailored pieces. A well-fitted outfit will make you look sharp while allowing you to feel comfortable and confident.

2. **COLOR:**
   The colors you wear shape the message you are sending through your attire. Different colors evoke different emotions, so understanding the psychology of color and

incorporating it into your wardrobe can help you to project your desired image.

3. **TEXTURE AND PATTERN:**
Mixing and matching different textures and patterns can add depth and interest to your outfit. However, you need to strike the right balance to maintain a polished look. Opt for subtle patterns and complementary textures that enhance your appearance without overpowering it.

4. **ACCESSORIES:**
The right accessories can elevate your outfit and showcase your style. Choose items that complement your attire and enhance your overall look, such as a statement necklace or a sleek leather belt. Remember, less is more when accessorizing for the workplace.

5. **PERSONAL BRAND:**
Your professional style should align with your brand and the image you want to project. Consider the impression you want to make on others and choose clothing that reflects your values, personality, and career goals.

Creating a powerful visual statement through your attire involves understanding and using all of these elements to your advantage. For example, as I prepared for that client meeting, I chose a well-fitted navy suit with a subtle pinstripe pattern, paired with a bold lime green camisole top that added a pop of color and communicated confidence. The sleek lines and sharp tailoring made me feel and look ready to take on anything. Every detail exuded professionalism and sophistication, from the crisp collar to the perfectly pressed trousers. As I walked into the meeting, I knew I was making the right impression — a statement of who I was and what I could achieve.

Personal branding plays a pivotal role in developing your professional wardrobe. Your attire is an extension of your brand, telling a story about who you are and what you represent. When you intentionally align your wardrobe choices with your brand, you create a cohesive image that resonates with others and helps you climb the ladder of success.

So, how do you begin to unveil your professional style? Start by assessing your current wardrobe and identifying any gaps or inconsistencies. Reflect on your brand and the image you want to project, and consciously align your clothing choices with those goals. Experiment with different colors, textures, and patterns, and observe how they influence the perceptions of people around you. Embrace the journey of self-discovery, and watch your look evolve to showcase your unique blend of power, influence, and presence.

> Be open to exploring new looks and experimenting with different wardrobe combinations, while staying true to your brand and values.
> —Michele Grant

The Benefits of Professional Style for Confidence, Credibility, and Respect

Confidence is a powerful tool in the workplace, and I realized early in my career that my attire could have an effect on my self-assurance. When you know you look good, it's easier to feel good, and that confidence shines through in everything you do. As you refine your professional style, you'll notice a positive shift in your self-esteem, which will, in turn, enhance your performance at work and your ability to command attention and respect from others.

Fashion is an applied art through which individuality can be expressed. Through the language of clothing, we can express our creativity, personality, and inner selves to the world. Attire has a profound ability to delineate and amplify our uniqueness. Research supports this notion: a study published in the 2014 *Journal of Experimental Social Psychology* by Galinsky Bauer, & Duarte, found that wearing formal clothing can increase feelings of empowerment and self-assurance.

Credibility is another asset when seeking to establish your professional brand. When you dress the part, you signal to others that you take your life's work and role seriously. A well-curated professional wardrobe can help you gain credibility among your colleagues and clients, leading to increased trust, greater influence, and accelerated career growth.

In the early days of my career, I quickly learned that dressing professionally was a key component of earning credibility, and my professional reputation grew as a result.

Finally, dressing professionally can earn you *respect* and *recognition*. Developing a solid approach to this communicates the idea that you are *prepared*, *capable*, and *invested* in your domain, which can lead others to view you as a *valuable asset* to the team. As you command respect through your *attire*, you'll find that doors begin to open, and you will get more *opportunities* to advance in your career.

Coco Chanel, renowned for her timeless style, once said, "Simplicity is the keynote of all true elegance." In my management engagement opportunities, I have had meetings with potential clients where this principle played a factor in conveying my experience and competence. With my simple yet elegant outfits, I showcased an unparalleled attention to detail. My classic and well-fitted attire was a testament to my good taste, and I consistently followed impeccable grooming routines that further demonstrated my dedication to presenting the best version of myself.

Clients recognized these qualities reflected in my appearance, which helped establish trust and rapport. They saw me as a reliable, skilled professional who would bring the same level of excellence to our partnerships. Ultimately, while my expertise earned the client's respect and secured a successful partnership, my adherence to the fundamentals of good dressing paved the way.

The Impact of Attire on First Impressions

The oft-repeated adage, "You never get a second chance to make a first impression" highlights the importance of presenting ourselves well at the outset of any interaction. In this section, we will explore the critical role that first impressions and attire play in establishing a solid initial perception and setting the stage for successful relationships in your field.

First impressions are formed in mere seconds, yet they can have a lasting effect on how others perceive and interact with us. According to a study by Princeton psychologists Janine Willis and Alexander Todorov, in the 2006 *Psychological Science* journal, it takes only a tenth of a second for people to form judgments about others based on their appearance. This underscores the importance

of dressing appropriately for any professional setting, as doing so can help to create a favorable initial perception.

The "halo effect" is a cognitive bias whereby an individual's overall positive impression of someone influences their judgment of that person's other traits, including competence, intelligence, and trustworthiness. Dressing well can create a halo effect, leading others to view you more favorably across various dimensions.

As I said, first impressions are often formed within seconds, and our clothing plays a significant role in shaping the way that others perceive us. Studies consistently show that individuals who are professionally dressed are typically perceived as more confident, successful, and of higher social status compared to individuals in casual attire. This phenomenon can be attributed to the way clothing acts as a visual cue, influencing the halo effect, where positive initial impressions lead to positive assumptions about other traits and abilities. This demonstrates the power of professional clothing in establishing a solid initial perception.

Research in the field of social psychology suggests that the clothing someone chooses to wear can greatly influence how they are perceived in terms of their expertise and reliability. Experiments indicate that when subjects were shown images of individuals depicted in formal business attire, they often rated them as more logical, efficient, and competent than those dressed in more casual clothing.

This further demonstrates the fact that our clothing is an intricate part of our identity. It acts as a visual resume, silently communicating our dedication, experience, and potential. Choosing clothing that mirrors the professional qualities we wish to exhibit establishes our position and reputation in any work setting.

Establishing a solid initial perception through your attire is the *first step* in building your professional image. To create lasting *impressions* and maintain the halo effect, you'll want to present yourself with consistent *professionalism* and *poise*.

"True elegance transcends immediate recognition and lingers in the memory. This perspective underscores the value of always dressing well, as doing so will help others remember you in a positive light and reinforce your professional image over time."

—Michele Grant

How Your Professional Image Affects Your Career

During my journey as a woman thriving in the corporate world, for over two decades, I've had the opportunity to break glass ceilings, challenge the status quo, and emerge as a leader in my field. All of this was made possible by my determination and the undeniable impact of my meticulously curated professional image.

I remember a pivotal moment in my career when I was up for a much-coveted management position. I needed an edge, something to make me stand out. That's when I took a chance and splurged on a beautifully tailored taupe suit with beige pinstripes, complete with a subtle ivory cowl neck blouse. As I strutted through the office, I couldn't help but notice the raised eyebrows and impressed glances from my colleagues. It was as if they were seeing me in a new light—and, in a way, they were. Even my boss, who could be quite the stoic, cracked a smile and quipped, "Ready to take over the world, are we?" I couldn't help but chuckle in response.

That day, I nailed the interview and ultimately clinched the promotion. It was a clear lesson in how my professional image could play an instrumental role in reshaping the perceptions others had of me. The suit wasn't just a garment but a symbol of my capability, ambition, and readiness to rise to the occasion.

Oscar Wilde once said, "You can never be overdressed or overeducated." This quote rings true when it comes to the workplace. A study conducted by researchers Adam D. Galinsky and Hajo Adam, published in the journal *Social Psychological and Personality Science*, explores the psychological effects of wearing formal clothing. Their research found that subjects wearing formal attire engaged in higher levels of abstract thinking compared to their casually dressed counterparts. This provides more evidence of how the way you dress can affect your cognitive processes, which in turn can affect professional results, including decision-making and problem-solving abilities. The implication is that dressing professionally can enhance an individual's mental functions in ways that are valued in professional situations, for instance during hiring, promotions, and raises. This demonstrates the undeniable influence that your professional image has on the opportunities available to you.

I once attended a networking event wearing a vibrant burnt orange dress that I had carefully chosen for its bold and empowering hue. Although it was a daring selection for me, I was amazed by the number of people who approached me, complimenting my outfit and striking up conversations. That night, I made several valuable connections that later led to business collaborations and opportunities. My decision to make a bold statement and be noticed created a lasting impression, allowing me to find greater ease in expanding my professional network and capitalizing on new opportunities.

> *Friends, cultivating a strong professional image is* not merely a superficial endeavor; it is a strategic investment in yourself. As the iconic fashion designer Diane von Furstenberg once said, "Style is something each of us already has; all we need to do is find it."
>
> —Michele Grant

The Path to Constructing a Professional Wardrobe

An intriguing example of the power of professional attire took place during a fast growth stage of my career. I was collaborating with a promising advertising technology client — a startup already generating remarkable revenues and gearing up for an IPO. My responsibility was to lead the digital strategy for their customer success portal, a critical component in solidifying their position as a company.

The client's dress code was more in line with a successful startup's casual, preppy vibe. I embraced their atmosphere by opting for a refined yet innovative ensemble that strayed from conventional business attire. My outfit struck the ideal balance between traditional and creative, mirroring the company's unicorn spirit.

Upon entering the weekly executive briefing, I sensed a palpable shift in energy due to my *wardrobe choice*. My presentation was well-received, and the client praised me for my strategic insights and my grasp of their unique company culture, which my wardrobe choice had helped *convey*.

To create a professional wardrobe that maximizes its potential, consider the following principles:

1. **UNDERSTAND YOUR ENVIRONMENT:**
   Dress to inspire and represent the company culture. As a consultant, adapting my wardrobe to suit the industry and working atmosphere has been very beneficial. For instance, when collaborating with luxury retail clients, I opt for elegant, upscale attire, while my wardrobe for tech clients leans towards a more modern and relaxed style.

2. **PRIORITIZE QUALITY:**
   A few carefully selected, high-quality items can make a difference. Investing in classic, well-fitted garments guarantees a wardrobe that stands the test of time. As fashion designer Vivienne Westwood wisely advised, "Buy less, choose well, make it last." This quote perfectly encapsulates the importance of focusing on quality over quantity when curating your professional wardrobe.

3. **EMBRACE VERSATILITY:**
   Create a wardrobe consisting of adaptable pieces that can be combined in various ways, enabling you to assemble outfits suitable for diverse professional settings. This approach not only optimizes your investment but also simplifies your morning routine.

4. **PAY ATTENTION TO THE DETAILS:**
   Accessories, such as jewelry, belts, and shoes, can add flair and finesse to your professional wardrobe. Be mindful of selecting items that enhance your overall outfit and contribute to a sense of confidence and composure.

Think of your wardrobe as a vibrant tapestry, each thread meticulously woven to tell a story of success. With every decision, from fabric to fit, you paint a picture of who you are and where you're headed.

> **"This isn't just about fitting in; it's about**
> weaving a vision of ambition, competence,
> and endless possibility. This tapestry, my friend,
> is yours to craft. Let's make it a masterpiece.
>
> **—Michele Grant**

• • •

In the next chapter, we will dive into dressing for your body type. By understanding the nuances of your shape, you'll be able to choose clothing that flatters yourW figure, creating balance and proportion. Together, we will explore tips and strategies for dressing to create a more elongated and streamlined silhouette and discuss the importance of fit and tailoring.

DRESSING FOR YOUR BODY TYPE: THE POWER DRESSER'S APPROACH

chapter 2

A few years ago, I was preparing for a client dinner and took my time carefully selecting attire that was flattering for my body type. My ensemble perfectly complemented my shape, creating a sense of balance and proportion that embodied confidence and elegance. As I dressed, I recalled the early days of uncertainty, when my outfits failed to represent my experience, exposure, and potential, leaving me feeling out of place and ill-prepared. With over 20 years of experience working with Fortune 500 firms across various industries, I had transformed my professional wardrobe and became a true Power Dresser by embracing my body type and using it to my advantage.

I also remember being invited to a charity gala; a black-tie event filled with the city's most influential figures. I often struggled to find clothing that properly fit my tall frame. I realized that my wardrobe consisted of pieces, whether it be dresses or pants, that needed to be longer to complement my body type. I knew that I needed to make a change and make adjustments. That night, wearing a stunning gown tailored to fit my tall frame, I felt radiant, poised, and genuinely at ease. This added to the many experiences that marked pivotal points of inspiration on my journey to mastering the art of dressing for my body type and exuding the presence of a true Power Dresser.

In this chapter, you will learn techniques to:

- **Identify your body type**
- **Choose clothing that flatters your shape**
- **Create balance and proportion in your outfit choices**
- **Understand the importance of fit and tailoring**

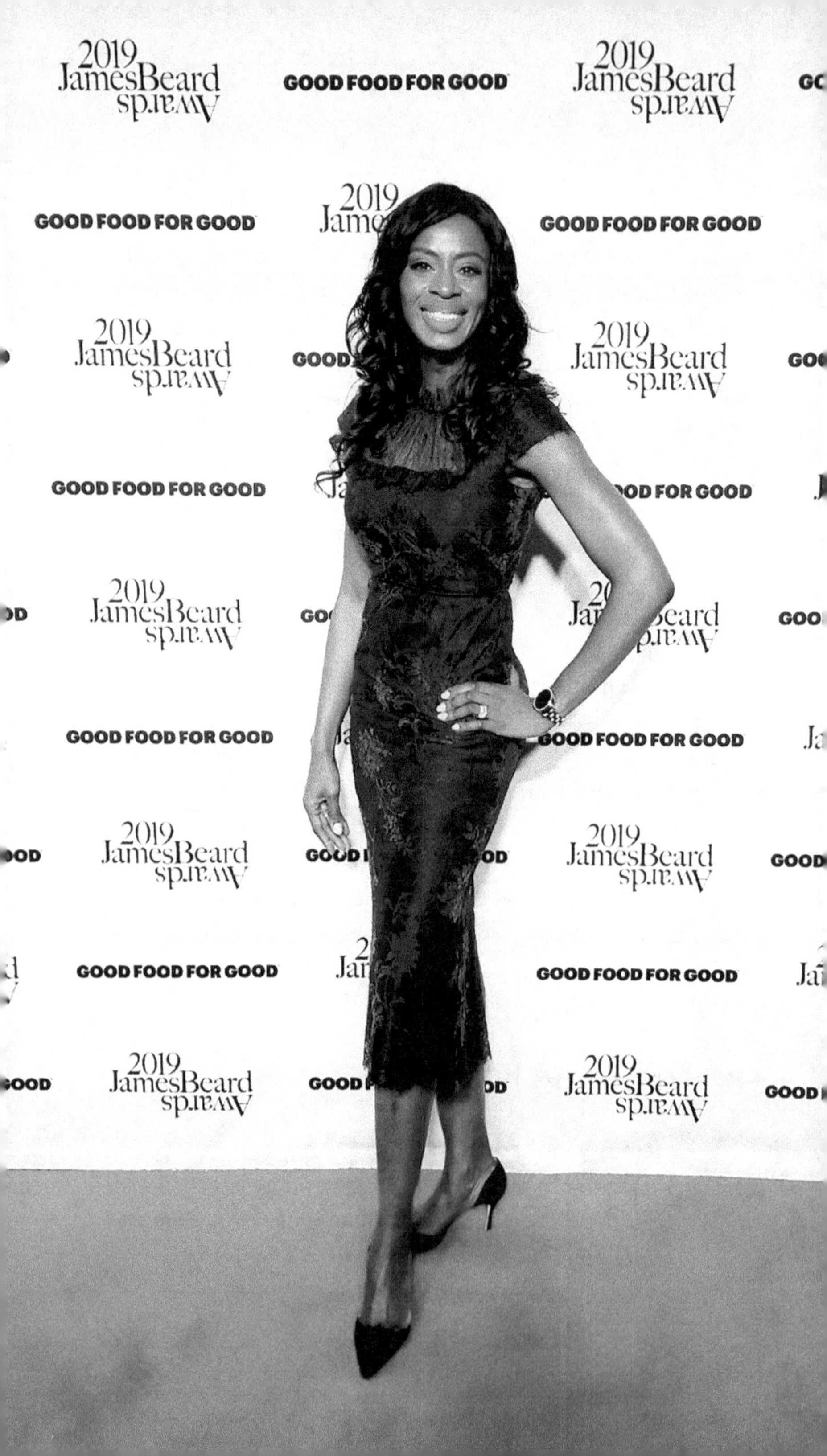
2019
JamesBeard
Awards
GOOD FOOD FOR GOOD

By understanding the unique nuances of your body type and how to dress to suit it, you can elevate your professional style and create a lasting impression on those around you. Join me as we delve into the Power Dresser's approach to dressing for your body type and unlocking the secrets to harnessing your wardrobe's full potential.

Identify Your Body Type

There isn't a one-size-fits-all solution when it comes to dressing professionally. Understanding your unique body type is key to creating a look that complements your strengths and minimizes your perceived flaws. As the celebrated fashion icon Coco Chanel once stated, "Fashion is architecture: it is a matter of proportions."

There are several commonly recognized body types, each with its own set of characteristics. While every individual is unique, most people can be put into one of the following categories:

1. **APPLE:**
   This body type is defined by a fuller waist and upper body, with narrower hips and thighs. Women with this shape often have a rounded tummy or fuller midsection. To create a more balanced silhouette, apple-shaped individuals can focus on clothing that highlights the shoulders, elongates the torso, and showcases the legs.

2. **PEAR:**
   The pear shape is characterized by a smaller bust and waist, with significantly wider hips. This body type, sometimes referred to as a "bottom-heavy" or "A-shaped" figure, can be enhanced by clothing that draws attention to the upper body and creates balance between the bust and hips.

3. RECTANGLE:
The rectangle body type has minimal curves, with the bust, waist, and hips being relatively equal in width. This shape, also known as a "straight" or "athletic" body type, is versatile when it comes to clothing choices, with the opportunity to create curves or maintain a streamlined silhouette.

4. HOURGLASS:
This body type is characterized by a well-defined waist, with the bust and hips being approximately the same width. The hourglass shape is often admired for its balanced proportions, allowing for a variety of clothing ensembles that can accentuate the natural curves.

5. INVERTED TRIANGLE:
Women with this body type typically have broader shoulders and a larger bust, which then narrows down to a smaller waist and hips. This shape, sometimes referred to as a "top-heavy" or "V-shaped" body type, can benefit from clothing that brings balance to the upper and lower body by emphasizing the waist or adding volume to the hips.

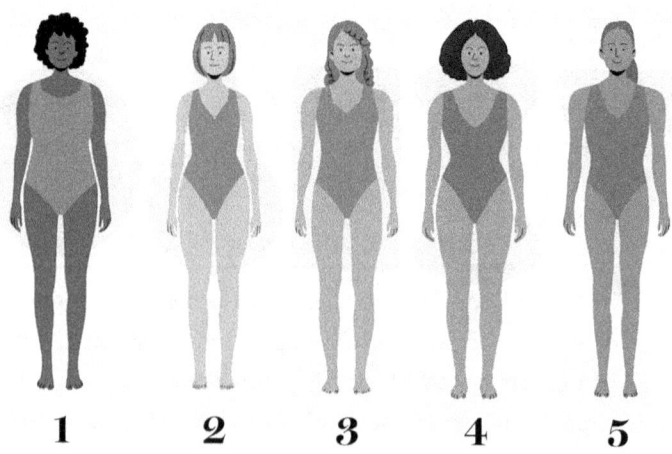

To determine your body type, you can measure the circumference of your bust, waist, and hips and compare the ratios. Alternatively, you can simply stand in front of a mirror and observe your natural silhouette. Remember, no body type is inherently better or worse than another; each has its own unique set of advantages and challenges when it comes to dressing professionally. It's also important to note that body types are not fixed categories. We don't always fit neatly into one specific type, as you may have characteristics from several different shapes. This variation is completely normal and offers even more versatility when selecting clothing that will complement your figure.

During my early days in the corporate world, selecting professional attire that enhanced my silhouette was challenging. It was when I definitively identified my body type as a rectangle that I was able to make informed choices about the garments that would work best for me. I discovered that selecting items with defined waistlines created the illusion of curves and projected a more balanced and elegant image. Armed with this knowledge, I began to gravitate towards shift dresses with strategic dart placements to introduce soft contours, A-line skirts that provided structure and visual interest, and high-waisted trousers that elongated my legs while offering the semblance of curves.

Interestingly, as I matured in my field, so did my silhouette. What was once a clearly defined rectangle began to soften and blossom, revealing a hint of an hourglass figure. While a dedicated fitness routine and a shift in dietary choices probably played a supporting role, I believe it was also the unfolding dance of time, shaping my form with the subtle brushstrokes of experience. This subtle transformation opened up a whole new world of fitting and styling possibilities.

I *embraced* bold waists with renewed *enthusiasm*, using them to celebrate my newfound *curves*. Fit-and-flare dresses became my allies, as their structured bodices and flowing skirts whispered *confidence* along with my new *contours*. Even my trusty shift dresses gained *playful* cinched waists, adding a touch of *elegance* and *whimsy* to my professional *persona*.

> **" This journey taught me that style is not static, but a dynamic dance between our evolving selves and the world around us.**
> **—Michele Grant "**

When you dress in a manner that flatters your body type, it can boost your self-esteem and make you feel more confident in your own skin. By identifying your body type and understanding its unique characteristics, you are well on your way to constructing a professional wardrobe that enhances and projects the image of a true Power Dresser.

Choose Clothing That Flatters Your Shape

When you dress in a way that complements your body shape, you showcase your strengths and make a powerful statement about who you are and what you bring to the table. To help you choose clothing that flatters your shape and highlights your best features, consider the following guidelines:

1. **APPLE:**
   Draw attention away from your fuller midsection by choosing clothing that elongates your torso and creates a more streamlined silhouette. Consider structured blazers that define your shoulders and draw the eye upward. Tailored tops that drape loosely around the midsection can be flattering, especially when paired with straight-leg trousers or pencil skirts that streamline the lower body.

V-necklines, empire waist dresses, and tunic tops are excellent choices for this body type. Opt for pants and skirts with a flat front, to minimize bulk in the waist area. Minimize the use of bulky fabrics and busy prints around the waist. The same applies to oversized or boxy tops that don't define your silhouette, as they can make your figure appear less structured.

PEAR:

Highlight your smaller waist by choosing clothing that accentuates this area, such as high-waisted pants and skirts or belted dresses. To balance your wider hips, opt for A-line skirts, straight-leg pants, and jackets that hit at the hip or slightly below. Look for tailored button-down shirts that tuck neatly into high-waisted trousers, creating a defined waistline. Structured jackets that end just below the waist can enhance this effect. Choose darker colors for your lower half with lighter or brighter blouses to draw attention upward. Avoid wearing tight, clingy bottoms that highlight the contrast between your hips and waist. In addition, be cautious with side pockets or embellishments on trousers or skirts that can add extra volume to your hips.

RECTANGLE:

Create the illusion of curves by choosing clothing that adds a bit of volume to your bust and hips. Peplum tops, A-line skirts, and darted shift dresses are ideal choices for this body type. You can also experiment with ruffles, frills, and other embellishments to add dimension to your figure. Choose blazers with nipped-in waists or princess seams to suggest curves. Trousers with pockets or patterns can give the illusion of wider hips. Avoid wearing overly baggy clothing that hides your shape completely. Clothes that are too tight may also emphasize the straightness of your silhouette instead of creating curves.

4. **HOURGLASS:**
Emphasize your well-defined waist by choosing clothing that cinches at the narrowest point. Wrap dresses, fitted blouses, and belted jackets are excellent options for this body type. Seek out sheath dresses with a slight stretch that hugs your curves, without being too tight. A well-fitted suit with a nipped-in waist can appropriately showcase your proportions in a work environment. Opt for tailored pants and pencil skirts that follow the natural curve of your hips and thighs. Avoid wearing clothing that is too loose and doesn't highlight your waist, as it can make you look shapeless. In addition, skirts and trousers that are too tight around the hips and thighs may be unprofessional and uncomfortable.

5. **INVERTED TRIANGLE:**
Balance your broader shoulders and larger bust by drawing attention to your waist and hips. Opt for V-necklines, flared skirts, and wide belts to create a more proportionate silhouette. Choose wide-leg pants or full skirts to balance your lower half with your upper body. Softly draped tops and tunics can soften the shoulder line. Be careful with garments that have shoulder pads or are too tight across the bust, as these can overemphasize your upper body. Tops with horizontal stripes across the shoulders may also create an overly broad effect.

Remember, these are just guidelines to help you begin exploring the best clothing options for your body type. Ultimately, the key to dressing for your shape is to be true to yourself, embrace your unique features, and wear clothing that makes you feel confident and assertive.

Create Balance and Proportion in Your Outfit Choices

Early in my journey as a Power Dresser, I remember being asked to speak at a conference in front of a large audience. I chose a visually top-heavy outfit, with a voluminous blouse and slim-fitting pants, which made my shoulders appear broader and accentuated my height, making me feel self-conscious on stage. That day, I discovered balance and proportion play a role in streamlining your silhouette, drawing attention to your best features, and ensuring that your outfit complements rather than overshadows your presence in a professional setting.

Creating balance and proportion in outfits is key to achieving a harmonious and stylish look. To achieve this, focus on fit by choosing pieces that flatter your body type and don't overwhelm your frame. Mixing and matching textures and patterns can add depth and interest to your outfit, while well-chosen accessories can tie everything together. Finally, consider the role of color in creating balance and harmony, and experiment with different combinations to find what works best for you. With these tips and a bit of experimentation, you can express yourself confidently and stylishly.

One strategy for creating balance is to consider the use of color-blocking. By choosing contrasting colors that work well together, you can create the illusion of balance and proportion, making your overall appearance more harmonious. For example, as I said, if you have a pear-shaped body, you might opt for a darker color on the bottom and a lighter color on the top, creating a visual balance between your hips and shoulders.

Another *technique* is to utilize patterns *strategically*. Bold patterns can draw the eye and create a *focal point*, while smaller patterns can help *balance* out areas that may seem more *prominent*. For instance, if you have an inverted triangle body shape, you could wear a plain top and a skirt or pants with a larger pattern, giving the appearance of a more *proportional silhouette*.

Choosing fitting silhouettes can also create balance and proportion. For example, if you have an apple-shaped body, you might choose a structured blazer with a nipped-in waist and a flowing skirt or wide-leg pants to create the appearance of a more defined waistline.

Don't be afraid to experiment and find what works best for your unique body shape. By taking the time to understand your body and make thoughtful choices in your wardrobe, you'll be well on your way to becoming a Power Dresser who understands the nuance and impact of every outfit choice.

Understand the Importance of Fit and Tailoring

> The dress must follow the body of a woman, not the body following the shape of the dress.
> –Hubert de Givenchy

Incorporating tailoring into your wardrobe strategy may seem like a luxury, but it is a worthy investment in your professional image. An outfit that fits like a glove speaks volumes about your commitment to excellence, both in how you present yourself and in your work. The famous designer Giorgio Armani once said, "To create something exceptional, your mindset must be relentlessly focused on the smallest detail."

To achieve a perfect fit, be sure to recognize when clothing may need tailoring. Here are some key indicators to help you determine when adjustments might be necessary:

1. **SHOULDER SEAMS:**
   The seams of your garment should align with the edge of your shoulders. If the seams are too far out, the item may appear oversized, while seams that are too close can make the garment feel restrictive.

2. **WAIST AND HIPS:**
   Properly fitted garments should follow the natural curve of your waist and hips without being too tight or loose. If you notice excessive fabric bunching or pulling, it may be time to consult a tailor.

3. **PANT LENGTH:**
   The hem of your pants should touch the top of your shoes, creating a slight break in the fabric. If your pants are too long, they may bunch at the bottom, while pants that are too short can appear ill-fitting and unprofessional.

4. **BLAZER FIT:**
   A well-fitted blazer should be snug but not tight across the chest and back, allowing for easy movement. If the blazer is too tight, the fabric may pull or gap, while a blazer that is too loose can appear boxy and shapeless.

5. **DRESS FIT:**
   A well-fitted dress should accentuate your best features, providing a flattering silhouette that is neither tight nor loose. Consider the following aspects when assessing the fit of a dress:

- **Bust:** The dress should fit comfortably across your bust without gaping or pulling.
- **Waist:** The waist should be accentuated without being restrictive.
- **Hip:** The dress should skim the hips without pulling or bunching.
- **Hem:** Aim for a hem that falls around the knee or slightly below, depending on the workplace and the specific style of the dress.
- **Sleeve** (if applicable): The sleeves should end just past the wrist bone.

If these elements are not correctly fitted, it may be time to consult a tailor. Seek a skilled tailor who understands your body type and can make the necessary adjustments. By investing in quality tailoring, you enhance your professional image and communicate your dedication to excellence and attention to detail.

Recognizing when your clothing may need tailoring is a skill worth honing to achieve that perfect fit. When the shoulder seams of a garment don't align with your shoulders, or if there's too much fabric bunching at the waist and hips, it's a clear sign that you should seek a tailor's expertise. Similarly, pant lengths that don't quite meet the top of your shoes (unless they are meant to be capris or cropped pants) or blazers that either gape or pull across the chest are all indicators of an ill-fitted wardrobe, but they are problems that a tailor can rectify.

Finding a skilled tailor is akin to finding a good mechanic; research and referrals go a long way. Once you've found a potential tailor, don't hesitate to ask for a consultation. It's your chance to discuss their approach. During fittings, be specific about what you want. If you can, bring an example of a similar piece that fits you perfectly.

> **Always provide feedback on the adjustments, ensuring they align with your comfort and desired style.**
> —Michele Grant

Standard tailoring adjustments, such as taking in or letting out seams, can revamp the fit around your body's curves, while hemming can adjust the length of your pants or skirts to just the right point. Sleeves that end just past the wrist bone and trousers that taper correctly can make your attire look bespoke.

The results of making these adjustments are manifold. Tailored clothes not only fit better but also move better with your body, enhancing both comfort and appearance. When clothes fit correctly, they tend to be worn more frequently, thus extending the life and wearability of your wardrobe.

Tailored clothing is the cornerstone of a polished professional look. It's worth investing time to find a good tailor, and clearly communicate your needs to them, to ensure each piece in your professional wardrobe is working its hardest for you.

Remember that a *well-tailored* outfit is a silent yet *powerful statement*. As the legendary Spanish fashion designer Cristóbal Balenciaga once said, "A *couturier* must be an *architect* for *plans*, a *sculptor* for *shapes*, an *artist* for *color*, a *musician* for *harmony* and a *philosopher* for the *sense of proportion*."

As we wrap up Chapter 2, it's clear that you can create a style that highlights your features by identifying your body type, choosing clothing that flatters you, establishing balance in your outfits, and paying attention to fit and tailoring.

• • •

In Chapter 3, we'll dive deeper into the fascinating world of color psychology and its influence on your professional style. We'll explore the importance of color in conveying confidence, authority, and sophistication, and learn how to thoughtfully incorporate both vibrant and subdued shades into your wardrobe. Additionally, we'll reveal strategies for skillfully combining colors to amplify your presence in various professional situations. So, let's continue to elevate your presence and refine your understanding of color in your wardrobe!

chapter 3

EMBRACING THE PSYCHOLOGY AND POWER OF COLOR IN PROFESSIONAL STYLE

There's an incredible power hidden within the colors we choose to wear. Color has the ability to evoke emotions, shape perceptions, and even influence the outcome of professional situations. Understanding the psychology behind color can elevate your aesthetic, boost how you are perceived, and attract opportunities as a Power Dresser.

This chapter will delve into the fascinating world of color, exploring its impact on our professional lives and explaining how to utilize it strategically in our wardrobe. From choosing colors that convey confidence, authority, and professionalism to incorporating bold hues and timeless neutrals, we will uncover the secrets to using color as a powerful tool for success.

The key topics we will cover in this chapter include:

- **Understanding the psychology of color in professional style**
- **Choosing colors that convey confidence, authority, and professionalism**
- **Incorporating bold colors into your wardrobe**
- **Selecting neutral colors to create a timeless, classic look**
- **Using color to dress for success in different professional situations**
- **Employing strategies for mixing and matching colors for maximum impact**

Understanding the Psychology of Color in Professional Style

Color has a profound psychological impact on our mood and perception, and even our behavior. As you cultivate your professional wardrobe, understanding the psychology of color can help you make more strategic and impactful choices that align with your desired message and persona.

Research has shown that colors can evoke strong emotional responses and influence decision-making. For instance, a comprehensive analysis on the influence of color in marketing from the 2015 Copenhagen Business School study by Sørensen & Kjeldsen highlights the way that various hues can trigger specific emotional responses. Studies such as these suggest that warm colors like red are often associated with excitement, while cool colors like blue can convey a sense of trustworthiness. Therefore, consider the colors you incorporate into your professional attire carefully.

Here are some insights into the psychological effects of various colors and how to leverage them accordingly:

1. **RED:**
   Red is a powerful, attention-grabbing color associated with energy, passion, and excitement. Wearing red can give you an air of confidence and assertiveness, making it an excellent choice for important meetings or presentations. However, be mindful of its intensity and opt for more subdued shades or accent pieces in more conservative settings.

2. **BLUE:**
   Blue is often associated with trustworthiness, stability, and calmness. It's a versatile color that can easily be incorporated

into your professional wardrobe, from navy suits to sky-blue blouses. Wearing blue can convey a sense of reliability and credibility, making it an ideal choice for job interviews and networking events.

GREEN:
Green has been linked to growth, balance, and harmony. This color can evoke a sense of calm and approachability, which can have benefits in collaborative work environments or team-building events. Consider wearing shades of green to signal your willingness to listen and work together effectively.

YELLOW:
Yellow is a vibrant color that can symbolize optimism, happiness, and creativity. While it might not be the most conventional choice for professional attire, incorporating yellow accessories or details can bring warmth and positivity to your look. Be cautious with the intensity of the shade, as excessively bright yellows can be overwhelming.

PURPLE:
Historically associated with royalty and luxury, purple can convey a sense of sophistication and creativity. Wearing shades of purple can communicate your innovative and ambitious nature, making it a great option for creative industries or leadership roles.

BLACK:
Black is a timeless, classic color often linked to power, elegance, and authority. A well-fitted black suit or dress can command attention and help you to exude confidence. However, be mindful of your message, as an all-black outfit may also come across as overly formal or unapproachable in certain settings.

The right *hue* can evoke the perfect *emotion* in professional settings. Mastering the art of combining colors in your wardrobe can make you stand out and create an *unforgettable presence*. Whether presenting to clients or mingling at a networking event, your color *choices* inform *perceptions*. A curated, yet personal array of hues projects *presence* and *charisma*. With discerning color sense, you can craft an image that *showcases* both your professional capabilities and your *distinctive style*.

Choosing Colors That Convey Confidence, Authority, and Professionalism

A key skill of Power Dressers is selecting the right colors to communicate confidence, authority, and professionalism. Understanding the psychological effects of colors and strategically incorporating them into your wardrobe can be powerful and invigorating.

Here are some color choices and tips to help you project a confident, authoritative, and professional image:

1. **CLASSIC NEUTRALS:**
   Colors like black, navy, and gray are timeless choices that can create a polished, professional look. These colors are often associated with stability, dependability, and authority. For example, a well-tailored navy suit can convey trustworthiness and competence, making it an excellent option for meetings or presentations.

2. **BOLD ACCENTS:**
   While sticking to a neutral palette is generally considered professional, incorporating bold colors through accessories or accent pieces can add a touch of individuality and self-assuredness to your look. Consider a statement necklace in a bold color or a vibrant scarf to showcase your unflappable assurance.

3. **COMPLEMENTARY SHADES:**
   Choose colors that harmonize with each other to create a cohesive and visually appealing outfit. For instance, pairing a deep burgundy blouse with a charcoal gray suit can convey a sense of sophistication and self-assurance. Utilizing a

color wheel can help you identify complementary colors and develop a well-balanced color palette for your wardrobe.

4. SKIN TONE CONSIDERATIONS:

Selecting colors that flatter your skin tone can enhance your overall appearance and boost your confidence. Generally, people with cool undertones (pink or blue) look best in cool colors such as blues, greens, and purples, while those with warm undertones (yellow or golden) are more suited to warmer hues like reds, oranges, and yellows. If you have warmer skin tones, you can even incorporate earthy tones such as olive green, mustard yellow, or burnt orange into your wardrobe. These colors not only complement your skin tone but also evoke a sense of warmth and approachability. Also, experiment with rich jewel tones like deep teal, emerald green, or burgundy, which can convey a sense of sophistication and power.

5. OCCASION-APPROPRIATE CHOICES:

It's crucial to consider the context and environment in which you will be wearing your chosen colors. For example, wearing a bold red dress to a job interview may not be the best choice, as it could come across as overly assertive or attention-seeking. Opt for more conservative colors in formal settings and reserve bold hues for networking events or creative industries.

The wise words of the trailblazing fashion icon Isaac Mizrahi remind us of the impact color can have on our emotional well-being and self-expression: "Color is like food for the spirit — plus it's not addictive or fattening." Power Dressers recognize the fact that the influence of color on our professional image is crucial. By thoughtfully selecting colors that exude confidence, authority,

and professionalism, we can make a memorable impact in any professional situation. When we harness the power of color and incorporate it into our wardrobe, we nourish our spirits and elevate our presence in the workplace.

Incorporating Bold Colors into Your Wardrobe

While it may initially feel intimidating, embracing vibrant hues can elevate your presence and inspire those around you. In the words of the influential color theorist Johannes Itten, "Color is life, for a world without color appears to us as dead." By confidently integrating bold colors into your professional wardrobe, you can breathe life into your style and make a powerful statement.

1. **START SMALL:**
   If you're new to wearing bold colors, begin by incorporating small pops of color into your outfits. This could be in the form of accessories like a statement necklace, a vibrant scarf, or colorful shoes. As you grow more comfortable, you can gradually introduce more color into your wardrobe through blouses, dresses, and jackets.

2. **PAIR WITH NEUTRALS:**
   To avoid feeling overwhelmed by bold colors, pair them with neutral hues such as black, white, or beige. For instance, you could wear a bright red blouse with a black pencil skirt or a pair of navy trousers with a striking yellow blazer. This will create a visually appealing balance between the bold and the understated.

CHOOSE FLATTERING COLORS:
Select bold colors that complement your skin tone and enhance your natural beauty. For example, if you favor a cooler palette, jewel tones like emerald green and royal blue will be particularly flattering. If you are drawn to warmer earthy tones, opt for earthy shades such as burnt orange or mustard yellow.

PLAY WITH PATTERNS:
Introduce bold colors through patterned clothing. This can be a subtler way to experiment with color, as the patterns will often incorporate both bold and neutral hues. Look for prints that include your chosen bold color, such as a floral blouse or a geometric dress.

CONSIDER COLOR-BLOCKING:
Color-blocking involves wearing two or more contrasting colors in a single outfit. This can be a stylish and sophisticated way to incorporate bold colors into your wardrobe. For example, pair a cobalt blue top with a bright pink skirt or a teal blazer with red trousers.

TRUST YOUR INSTINCTS:
The most important aspect of incorporating bold colors into your wardrobe is trusting your instincts. As Coco Chanel once said, "The best color in the world is the one that looks good on you." Experiment with different hues and pay attention to how they make you feel. Choose colors that bring out your confidence and make you feel unstoppable.

True Power Dressers wield color as a strategic tool, using cleverly calculated color palettes that project dynamism, creativity, and innovative thinking. By embracing a signature color or two in their professional wardrobes, Power Dressers stand poised to dominate any room they enter, and thus influence perceptions. Their bold yet thoughtful chromatic choices reflect the potency of their ideas while conveying individuality. Both daring and strategic, this use of color complements their credentials and announces their presence before words are even spoken. Deliberate color palettes are more than just fashion-forward; they also exude an unmistakable aura — one that catalyzes connections and affirms authority wherever they go. For the modern mover and shaker, color is a dependable ally in achieving impact.

Selecting Neutral Colors to Create a Timeless and Classic Look

> **"**
> **Neutrals are not boring; they are the canvas of your power.**
> **—Michele Grant**
> **"**

Selecting neutral colors to create a timeless and classic look is a winning skill for any Power Dresser. By serving as a versatile foundation for your attire, neutrals facilitate effortless mixing and matching. Rather than fade into the backdrop, harness neutrals to highlight your own depth and dimension. The right ecru, tan, or slate grey not only blends effortlessly into any setting, but also spotlights your personal complexity. Savvy incorporation of neutrals crafts a versatile image that mingles friendliness and authority, while keeping focus on your talents and capabilities.

1. **KNOW YOUR NEUTRALS:**
Neutral colors include shades of black, white, gray, beige, and navy. These colors are considered timeless because they don't go out of style and can be easily paired with other colors, patterns, or textures. Building your wardrobe with neutral pieces ensures your clothing remains fashionable and versatile.

2. **INVEST IN QUALITY STAPLES:**
Look for high-quality staple pieces that stand the test of time. This may include a well-fitting black blazer, a crisp white button-down shirt or silk blouse, tailored trousers in gray or navy, and a camel-colored coat. These items can be mixed and matched to create several outfit combinations, making them invaluable additions to your wardrobe.

3. **PLAY WITH TEXTURE:** i
Incorporate different textures to add depth and visual interest to your neutral outfits. For example, you could wear a silk blouse with a tweed skirt or a cashmere sweater with a leather pencil skirt. Mixing textures can elevate a neutral outfit and create a sophisticated, multidimensional look.

4. **EXPERIMENT WITH PATTERNS:**
While neutral colors may be the primary focus of your outfit, you can still introduce patterns to create visual interest. Look for subtle patterns that incorporate neutral colors, like pinstripes, houndstooth, or herringbone. This can add an element of intrigue to your outfit while maintaining its timeless appeal.

5\. **OPT FOR MONOCHROMATIC OUTFITS:**
Wearing a single color from head to toe can create a chic and streamlined appearance. Monochromatic outfits can be particularly effective when using neutral colors, as they exude elegance and sophistication. For example, try wearing an all-black ensemble with a black blazer, blouse, and trousers, or go for an all-white look with a white dress and coordinating accessories.

6\. **CONSIDER THE ROLE OF ACCESSORIES:**
The key to making a neutral outfit stand out lies in the details. Thoughtfully selected accessories can communicate poise and certitude. Invest in high-quality belts, bags, and shoes that complement your neutral wardrobe. Choose distinctive and polished accessories with tactile textures or subtle embellishments to add depth and personality to your outfit. More to come on these suggestions later on in the book!

As you embrace the art of power dressing, remember the words of legendary fashion editor Diana Vreeland: "Style — all who have it share one thing: originality." You can create a truly original and memorable professional wardrobe by skillfully combining neutral colors with thoughtful touches of patterns and accessories.

Using Color to Dress for Success in Different Professional Situations

Navigating the nuances of dressing for different professional situations can be a daunting task, especially when it comes to selecting the right colors. Let's explore some different settings in which hues can influence how you are perceived by your colleagues and superiors.

1 **JOB INTERVIEWS:**
Choosing the appropriate colors for a job interview is an easy way to showcase your professionalism and confidence. Opt for conservative colors like navy blue, black, or charcoal gray, which convey reliability and competence. Adding a subtle pop of color with a blouse or scarf can make you memorable without overwhelming the interviewer.

2 **BUSINESS MEETINGS:**
In high-stakes situations like board meetings or presentations, it's crucial to project authority and trustworthiness. Opt for darker, solid colors such as navy or charcoal, which command respect, and pair them with lighter-colored shirts or blouses for contrast. This combination can make you appear more approachable and open to collaboration.

3 **NETWORKING EVENTS:**
When attending professional networking events, consider wearing colors that express confidence and energy. Shades of red, orange, or purple can help you stand out in a crowd and make a lasting impression on new connections. However, be mindful of the event's tone and dress code, and ensure your choices are appropriate for the occasion.

4 **CASUAL FRIDAYS:**
Some workplaces have more relaxed dress codes on Fridays, allowing employees to play with trends and take a more artful approach to their clothes. On these days, feel free to experiment with bolder colors and prints, but maintain a professional appearance by pairing them with neutral-colored bottoms or outerwear.

5 CLIENT MEETINGS:
When meeting with clients, strike a balance between approachability and authority. Choose colors that demonstrate your reliability and expertise, such as deep forest green or charcoal gray. Feel free to incorporate softer hues like pastels or jewel tones to project warmth and openness.

6 VIRTUAL MEETINGS:
In a digital work environment, colors can appear differently on screens, so it's crucial to consider how your attire will translate on camera. Stick to solid, bold colors that contrast nicely with your background, and avoid busy patterns or stripes that can create visual distractions.

7 TEAM-BUILDING EVENTS:
When attending team building or company retreats, you can opt for more relaxed, approachable colors. Pastels and earth tones can convey a sense of warmth and camaraderie, helping to foster connections with your colleagues.

8 CHARITY EVENTS AND FUNDRAISERS:
At professional events with a philanthropic focus, wearing softer colors like sky-blue, lavender, and blush can demonstrate your sensitivity and empathy towards the cause. They can create a welcoming atmosphere and encourage open conversations with other attendees.

As the renowned artist Georgia O'Keeffe once said, "I found I could say things with color and shapes that I couldn't say any other way." By thoughtfully selecting your color palette for different situations, you can communicate your desired message and create meaningful connections with those around you.

Employing Strategies for Mixing and Matching Colors for Maximum Impact

Playing with color is a way to express our emotions, our creativity, and our uniqueness in the workplace. Don't be afraid to make a statement with the colors you choose; they can help tell the world who you are and what you stand for.

As you venture into the world of color, mixing and matching can be an exciting yet uncertain process. But fear not, The Power Dressers' Color Palette is here to guide your steps and elevate your professional wardrobe. We'll look at it in more detail soon, but first, let's explore some invaluable techniques to make the most of this curated palette.

1. **KNOW YOUR COLOR ALLIES AND LEVERAGE THE COLOR WHEEL:**
   Familiarity with the color wheel and The Power Dressers' Color Palette is your compass. Complementary colors like fiery red and cool teal, drawn from opposite sides of the color wheel, ignite bold statements. Analogous pairs of color (pairs that are adjacent to each other on the color wheel), such as deep navy and vibrant turquoise, weave harmonious looks with subtle contrasts. Explore, experiment, and see what resonates with your mood!

2. **CRAFT YOUR PERSONAL PALETTE:**
   Discover the hues that flatter your skin tone, hair, and eyes. Building a wardrobe around these colors, your Power Palette as we call it, becomes an effortless way to radiate confidence and polish. Use your palette as a foundation, then branch out with adventurous accents from The Power Dressers' Color Palette for dynamic outfits.

3. **THE 60-30-10 RULE:**
   Imagine your outfit as a canvas. Allocate 60 percent to a dominant color, perhaps a deep emerald green from your palette. Fill 30 percent with a supporting shade, like a complementary touch of plum from the wider palette. Finally, add a final flourish with 10 percent of an accent color, like a vibrant lime green from your personal hues. This formula ensures balance and cohesion, while crafting signature ensembles.

4. **EXPERIMENT WITH ANALOGOUS COLORS FOR EFFORTLESS SOPHISTICATION:**
   Neighboring colors on the wheel sing in perfect harmony. Try pairing a rich cobalt blue from your palette with a shimmering teal from The Power Dressers' Color Palette for a visually pleasing and professional ensemble. Remember, analogous combinations lend themselves to endless variations within your personal color choices.

5. **EXPLORE TRIADIC COLORS FOR DYNAMIC ELEGANCE:**
   Explore the magic of three! Triadic color schemes involve combining colors evenly spaced on the wheel, like navy blue, burgundy, and dark forest green. This sophisticated arrangement, found within your palette and the expanded options, offers richness, depth, and a dynamic visual appeal perfect for the boardroom.

6. **EMBRACE THE BOLDNESS OF COLOR-BLOCKING FOR FEARLESS FUSION:**
   Let two or more solid colors from your palette or wider selection take center stage! For a modern edge, choose colors with similar intensity levels, like a fiery orange next to a vibrant coral. Or, delve into the world of complementary

or triadic combinations for a high-contrast statement. Remember, confidence is your ultimate accessory when rocking this technique.

7. LET TEMPERATURE GUIDE YOU:

Pay attention to the undertones of each color, whether warm (think golden yellow) or cool (imagine emerald green). Combining both can create an intriguing contrast, while sticking to one temperature family fosters a sense of calm and harmony. Use your Power Dresser's Color Palette as a guide to explore both options and discover what flatters your unique style.

8. ACCENT WITH METALLICS:

Gold, silver, and bronze, found in The Power Dressers' Color Palette, can be your chameleon companions. Use them as versatile neutrals to ground a vibrant outfit or as bold accents to add instant sophistication. Imagine a sleek silver belt cinching a royal blue dress or a touch of gold jewelry complementing a rich plum ensemble.

9. FIND INSPIRATION IN NATURE'S PALETTE:

Look around you! Nature's tapestry of colors offers endless inspiration. A fiery sunset's blend of orange and purple can translate into a statement blouse and skirt combination from your palette. A blooming garden's symphony of greens and pinks might whisper the idea of a tailored sage green suit adorned with a delicate pink scarf. Let the world guide your creativity and infuse your professional attire with natural elegance.

The Power Dressers' Color Palette is your key to ***crafting outfits*** that not only elevate your style, but also ***speak volumes*** about your personality. Forget one-dimensional wardrobes – this ***vibrant guide*** empowers you to mix and match ***bold hues***, explore ***harmonious blends***, and unleash your inner power through the ***language of color***.

The Power Dressers' Color Palette

Base Color	Accent Colors			Neutral Colors (Note: Pearls can be added to any combination)
	Complementary Color	Analogous Colors	Triadic Colors	
Burnt Orange	Teal	Coral, Terracotta	Olive Green, Violet	Charcoal Gray, Camel, Brown, Gold
Cherry Red	Emerald Green	Cranberry, Crimson	Teal, Sage Green	White, Black, Brown, Silver
Coral	Turquoise	Pink Coral, Salmon	Seafoam Green, Lavender	Ivory, Taupe, Nude, Soft Gold
Crimson	Green	Maroon, Magenta	Navy Blue, Kelly Green	Charcoal Gray, Taupe, Black, Silver
Light Denim Blue	Peach	Periwinkle, Dusty Blue	Pale Coral, Light Yellow-Green	White, Camel, Nude, Silver
Dusty Peach	Seafoam Green	Blush, Apricot	Lilac, Soft Green	Light Gray, Beige, Brown, Soft Gold
Dusty Pink	Olive Green	Mauve, Rose	Pale Green, Light Blue	Cream, White, Nude, Rose Gold
Eggplant	Yellow-Green	Aubergine, Plum	Forest Green, Sienna	Charcoal Gray, Black, Brown, Silver
Emerald Green	Red	Hunter Green, Seafoam Green	Amethyst Purple, Ruby Red	White, Cream, Black, Gold
Fuchsia	Green	Magenta, Violet	Lime Green, Cyan	Black, White, Gray, Gold

The Power Dressers' Color Palette

Base Color	Accent Colors			Neutral Colors (Note: Pearls can be added to any combination)
	Complementary Color	Analogous Colors	Triadic Colors	
Lavender	Pastel Yellow	Pale Lavender, Lilac	Light Green, Pastel Yellow	Gray, Taupe, Nude, Silver
Maroon	Turquoise	Burgundy, Wine Red	Navy Blue, Dark Green	Ivory, Mushroom, Black, Gold
Mauve	Yellow Green	Dusty Lavender, Violet	Teal, Olive Green	Taupe, Light Gray, Nude, Bronze
Mint Green	Red Violet	Seafoam Green, Lime Green	Lavender, Soft Pink	Beige, White, Gray, Silver
Mustard Yellow	Violet	Coral, Chartreuse	Navy Blue, Teal	Brown, Khaki, Gray, Bronze
Navy Blue	Rust	Royal Blue, Midnight Blue	Dark Green, Maroon	White, Cream, Gray, Silver
Olive Green	Magenta	Sage Green, Teal	Plum, Orange-Yellow	Khaki, Tan, Brown, Gold
Pink	Sage Green	Rose, Coral	Light Blue, Light Green	Ivory, White, Gray, Rose Gold
Royal Blue	Orange Yellow	Navy Blue, Cobalt Blue	Orange Red, Hot Pink	White, Light Gray, Black, Silver
Violet	Lime Green	Lavender, Magenta	Blue Green, Red Orange	Black, Gray, White, Silver

Embracing the Psychology and Power of Color in Professional Style

Dive into the "Base," "Accents," and "Accessories" sections below, and discover how to transform a garment into a statement, a blouse into a declaration, and every accessory into a brushstroke of your unique personality.

1 BASE:

- **Select a primary color:**
  - This is the star of the show! Browse the **Base Color** column and choose a shade that speaks to you, whether it's the vibrant Burnt Orange, the sophisticated Cherry Red, or the elegant Dusty Pink.

- **Pick your key piece:**
  - Decide which wardrobe cornerstone you want to wear to showcase your chosen color. Will it be a commanding dress, a tailored blazer, a flattering pair of pants, or a flowing skirt?

- **Consider neutral foundations:**
  - For a versatile base, opt for a neutral piece (pants, skirt, blazer, or dress) in a shade from the **Neutral Colors** column that complements your base color's undertones. This allows you easily to experiment with different color combinations.

2 ACCENTS:

- **Color Scheme Options:** Now, the fun part! Choose your supporting cast of colors in three different ways:
  - Dive into the **Complementary Color** column for a bold, eye-catching statement. Pair Burnt Orange with

Teal for a dynamic contrast, Cherry Red with Emerald Green for a luxurious vibe, or Dusty Pink with Olive Green for a serene balance.
  - Keep things harmonious with the **Analogous Colors** column. Coral, Terracotta, and Salmon would beautifully complement Burnt Orange, while Cranberry, Crimson, and Magenta can add depth to Cherry Red. For Dusty Pink, explore Blush, Apricot, and Mauve for a soft and romantic feel.
  - For a vibrant splash of variety, use the **Triadic Colors** column. Olive Green and Violet will add intrigue to Burnt Orange, Teal and Chartreuse offer a playful twist to Cherry Red, and Pale Green and Light Blue can soften Dusty Pink.

- **Incorporate neutral accents:** Balance bold colors or patterns with neutral accessories (belts, jewelry, shoes) from the **Neutral Colors** column to create harmony.

ACCESSORIES:

- **Unify with color scheme:**
  - Choose accessories (jewelry, belts, handbags, shoes) that align with your chosen color scheme to create a cohesive look.
  - When selecting colors from your palette, consider the type of accessory you will use, and its visual effects.

- **Accentuate with personality:**
  - Incorporate an accent color from your palette into select accessories to add a vibrant touch that reflects your unique style.

- Strategically choose which accessory will showcase the accent color to create a balanced, yet eye-catching effect.

- **Balance with neutrals:**
  - Utilize neutral accessories (belts, jewelry, shoes) to create harmony, temper boldness, and highlight professionalism.
  - Consider the visual weight of the neutral accessory and how it interacts with other elements of your outfit.

- **Expand versatility:**
  - Neutral accessories can effortlessly transition between different color schemes, maximizing your wardrobe's potential.
  - Invest in high-quality neutral pieces that can be mixed and matched with various color combinations.

Here are a few bold and invigorating examples to get your creative juices flowing!

Royal Authority:

- **Base:** royal blue tailored blazer
- **Accent:** white blouse, navy blue skirt
- **Accessories:** silver jewelry, navy pumps, and bag

Empowered Elegance:

- **Base:** mustard yellow wide-leg jumpsuit
- **Accent:** teal neck scarf
- **Accessories:** gold jewelry, brown heels, and bag

Strategic Simplicity:

- **Base:** ivory silk blouse
- **Accent:** charcoal gray tailored pants
- **Accessories:** gold jewelry, black belt, loafers, and bag

Confident Creativity:

- **Base:** fuchsia leather dress
- **Accent:** green silk scarf
- **Accessories:** silver jewelry, black open-toe heels, and bag

Polished Professional:

- **Base:** mauve jacquard trousers
- **Accent:** light gray silk blouse
- **Accessories:** bronze jewelry, taupe belt, heels, and bag

Inspired Innovation:

- **Base:** emerald green knit cardigan
- **Accent:** ruby red silk camisole, cream pants
- **Accessories:** gold jewelry, black belt, heels, and emerald green bag

Modern Muse:

- **Base:** dusty pink midi dress
- **Accent:** sage green pashmina scarf
- **Accessories:** rose gold jewelry, taupe heels, and bag

Cool Confidence:

- **Base:** navy blue turtleneck
- **Accent:** charcoal gray pants and blazer
- **Accessories:** silver jewelry, black patent leather belt, and kitten heels

Executive Edge:

- **Base:** olive green tailored blazer
- **Accent:** magenta silk camisole, tan trousers
- **Accessories:** bronze jewelry, cognac loafers, and bag

City Chic:

- **Base:** light denim jeans
- **Accent:** dusty peach silk camisole, white blazer
- **Accessories:** silver jewelry, white flats, and bag

Artistic Flair:

- **Base:** lavender tweed dress
- **Accent:** magenta scarf
- **Accessories:** pearl jewelry, black kitten heels

Creative Visionary:

- **Base:** cherry red dress
- **Accent:** sage green cardigan
- **Accessories:** silver jewelry, brown sandal heels and bag

The polished business professional understands that color projects and nonverbal cues are essential for positioning, and for influencing others. A bold crimson commands attention amid a sea of navy suits, immediately signaling confidence and authority. Contrast feminine hues like sage green with sharp tailoring to exhibit both warmth and decisiveness. Even all-black, when intentionally assembled, demonstrates control and seriousness. Your judiciously chosen color combination arises not from a trend but from strategy, airing traits through aesthetic articulation. In this visual language, you compose an empowered form of diplomacy that asserts leadership. The colors you wear will change the conversation, redirecting focus to your goals even before you discuss them.

> **Utilize this phenomenon to your advantage as you steer outcomes through intentional color messaging.**
> **—Michele Grant**

By incorporating these new and unique strategies while wielding The Power Dressers' Color Palette as your trusty tool, you'll transform your professional wardrobe into a canvas of confidence and power. Remember, color is a language, and your outfits become your story. Speak it boldly, own it authentically, and remember — the key is to experiment, have fun, and let your personality shine through your color choices.

As we reflect on the journey we've taken in Chapter 3, it's clear that color plays an integral role in our professional dressing, shaping our emotions and the perceptions of others. We've learned to harness the power of color strategically, blending bold hues and timeless neutrals to craft a wardrobe that exudes authority and professionalism.

• • •

Let's continue to evolve these concepts and deepen our understanding of what it means to be Power Dressers by considering the wider impact of our fashion choices. In the upcoming chapter, we'll take a thoughtful approach to curating a leader's wardrobe that embraces both sustainability and style. We'll delve into the world of ethical fashion, learn to identify planet-friendly elements, discover intentional shopping strategies, and organize a wardrobe that reflects our values. By merging our fashion persona with responsible choices, we'll make a meaningful difference that resonates with our aspirations and contributes to a more sustainable future.

chapter 4

BUILDING A PROFESSIONAL WARDROBE WITH SUSTAINABILITY AND STYLE IN MIND

The more we aim to become Power Dressers, the more we see that there are practical, as well as aesthetic considerations behind what we wear. In a world where ethical and sustainable practices are becoming more important, it is natural to think about the way our clothing choices will affect society and the environment. This chapter will show you how to exercise fashion for good and put together an environmentally conscious changemaker's wardrobe that won't break the bank.

In this chapter, we'll cover topics such as:

- **Understanding sustainable and ethical fashion practices**
- **Identifying your personal style while prioritizing eco-conscious and ethical choices**
- **Shopping strategies for finding quality, sustainable items that elevate your style**
- **Maintaining and organizing your wardrobe for long-lasting, sustainable use**
- **Balancing sustainability, style, and budget when building your professional wardrobe**

Understanding Sustainable and Ethical Fashion Practices

Sustainable fashion refers to the design, production, and consumption of clothing in a manner that minimizes negative environmental impacts and promotes social justice. Ethical fashion, on the other hand, primarily focuses on the fair treatment of workers throughout the supply chain, from raw material production to retail. By incorporating both aspects into your wardrobe choices, you can cultivate a style that radiates strength, sophistication, and responsibility, reflecting your mindful engagement with the world around you.

The main points to consider include:

1. **THE ENVIRONMENTAL IMPACT OF FASHION:**
   The fashion industry is one of the largest polluters globally, contributing to water pollution, greenhouse gas emissions, and excessive waste. According to the 2017 Ellen MacArthur Foundation report, the fashion industry produces approximately 10% of global greenhouse gas emissions, surpassing the combined emissions of all international flights and maritime shipping. Choosing eco-conscious fashion options reduces your environmental footprint and promotes eco-friendly practices.

2. **FAIR LABOR PRACTICES AND WORKER WELFARE:**
   Ethical fashion ensures that workers throughout the supply chain are paid fair wages, in safe conditions, and are treated with dignity and respect. As fashion journalist Lucy Siegle poignantly writes, "Fast fashion isn't free. Someone, somewhere is paying." We need to think about the human and environmental cost of what we wear. By supporting

ethical fashion brands, you can use your wallet to vote and advocate for fair labor practices.

3 **MATERIALS AND PRODUCTION METHODS:**
Sustainable and ethical fashion practices emphasize the use of eco-friendly materials, such as organic cotton, Tencel, and recycled fibers, as well as innovative production techniques that reduce waste and energy consumption. According to the Global Fashion Agenda's 2018 *Pulse of the Fashion Industry* report, switching to more planet-friendly materials could markedly reduce the fashion industry's environmental impact.

4 **TRANSPARENCY AND TRACEABILITY:**
In order to make smart choices, it is important to know where your clothes come from, and how they were made. Many environmentally friendly brands are committed to transparency, providing information about their supply chain, materials, and production methods. You can use resources like the Fashion Transparency Index and the Good On You app to evaluate brands.

To begin incorporating these practices into your professional wardrobe, consider the following steps:

1 Educate yourself about the environmental and social impact of the fashion industry.

2 Research brands that prioritize these practices.

3 Choose clothing made from eco-friendly materials and produced through responsible methods.

4. Prioritize quality over quantity, investing in timeless pieces that will last.

5. Support transparent brands that share information about their supply chain and labor practices.

Building a wardrobe aligned with these practices isn't just about fashion; it's also about taking a stand for a world that works for everyone.

> " Every ethical or environmentally conscious piece you choose becomes a vote for a more just and climate-positive future.
> —Michele Grant "

Identifying Your Personal Style While Prioritizing Eco-Conscious and Ethical Choices

Developing your style while prioritizing eco-conscious and ethical practices requires a thoughtful approach that balances your aesthetic preferences and values. These choices will reflect your commitment to a better future, while showcasing your taste and creativity.

1. REFLECT ON YOUR VALUES AND WHAT MATTERS TO YOU:
Before you start defining your eco-conscious personal style, take a moment to consider what this means to you. Are you passionate about reducing waste and using resources efficiently? Do you prioritize supporting brands that promote fair labor practices and pay their workers living wages? Understanding your values will help guide your choices as you build your wardrobe.

2. RESEARCH BRANDS AND MATERIALS:
To create a wardrobe that aligns with your values, familiarize yourself with brands known for their eco-conscious practices. Look for companies prioritizing transparency, and sharing information about their manufacturing processes, materials, and labor practices. Additionally, research materials such as organic cotton, Tencel, and recycled fabrics, and consider incorporating them into your wardrobe.

3. CHOOSE TIMELESS, VERSATILE PIECES:
Focus on timeless, versatile pieces that can be worn in various settings and combinations. Investing in high-quality, durable, and fashionable items can reduce waste and ensure your wardrobe remains relevant.

4. EMBRACE SLOW FASHION:
Slow fashion is an approach that prioritizes high-quality, low-impact, responsible practices over the rapid consumption and disposal of clothing. Keep eco-consciousness in mind, and seek brands that adhere to slow fashion principles. By choosing items that are designed to last, made from durable materials, and produced ethically, you'll be able to build a wardrobe that seeks to better our environment.

5. **UPCYCLE AND CUSTOMIZE:**
Upcycling involves repurposing or modifying existing clothing items to give them new life, adding a personal touch to your wardrobe while reducing waste. You can upcycle garments by altering their shape, size, or design, or combining elements from different items to create something new. Customizing your clothes is another way to express your individuality while staying eco-conscious. Adding embroidery, patches, or other embellishments to your existing garments can create a unique look and extend their life, all while keeping sustainability in mind.

6. **CHOOSE NATURAL AND SUSTAINABLE FABRICS:**
When building your eco-conscious wardrobe, prioritize natural, recycled, and biodegradable fabrics. Materials like organic cotton, linen, Tencel, and bamboo are more environmentally friendly than synthetic materials, which are often derived from petroleum-based processes. Additionally, these natural fabrics tend to be more breathable and comfortable.

As Stella McCartney, an advocate for sustainable fashion, once said, "Everyone can do simple things to make a difference, and every little bit really does count." Your eco-conscious decisions can make a statement about your commitment to a better future, while showcasing your taste and creativity.

Craft your trailblazing wardrobe with the same precision you bring to your boardroom strategies. Begin by unveiling your core values, then seek out brands that echo your ethical aspirations. Invest in high-quality pieces designed to withstand the test of time and add personalized touches that speak volumes about your individuality.

Through this process, you'll create a wardrobe that not only *empowers you*, but also *contributes* to a more responsible and *stylish future*. Remember, in this realm of power dressing, every garment becomes a *statement*, whispering your *values* and *inspiring* others to follow suit.

Shopping Strategies for Finding Quality, Sustainable Items That Elevate Your Style

During a recent networking event, I wore an elegant, tailored tuxedo V-neck jumpsuit made from organic cotton. The piece was designed by an up-and-coming sustainable brand that focused on using eco-friendly materials and prioritizing fair labor practices. The bold yet sophisticated design of the jumpsuit, combined with its planet-friendly origins, made it stand out in the sea of traditional professional attire. Several attendees admired the selection, asking where I had found such a well-fitted and elegant piece. Selecting that particular garment gave me the perfect opportunity to share my commitment to eco-conscious fashion choices. Those brief exchanges sparked meaningful conversations about shared values, and eventually led to a fruitful collaboration.

Building a repertoire of stylish and responsible pieces can be an enlightening and satisfying experience. Here are some innovative and effective shopping strategies to help you find sustainable pieces:

1. **RESEARCH BRANDS AND CERTIFICATIONS:**
   Before shopping, familiarize yourself with sustainable and ethical fashion brands. Look for certifications like Fair Trade, GOTS (Global Organic Textile Standard), and B Corp, which indicate a commitment to social and environmental responsibility. As Mary Creagh MP, Chair of the Fashion Revolution Environmental Audit Committee, said: "Fashion shouldn't cost the earth. But the way we design, make and discard clothes has a huge environmental impact." By choosing brands that prioritize sustainability, you are making an intentional effort to support these practices in the fashion industry.

SHOP SECONDHAND AND VINTAGE:
Shopping for pre-loved clothing is an excellent way to find unique and stylish items while reducing environmental impact. Thrift stores, consignment shops, and online platforms like Poshmark or The RealReal offer a wide variety of sustainable and high-quality pieces, at a fraction of the cost of new items.

PRIORITIZE TIMELESS, VERSATILE PIECES:
Invest in versatile, classic items that can be easily mixed and matched to create various outfits. As Orsola de Castro wisely states, "The most sustainable garment is the one already in your wardrobe." This reduces the need for excessive clothing and ensures that your wardrobe remains stylish and relevant over time.

EXPLORE CLOTHING RENTAL SERVICES:
With the rise of the sharing economy, several clothing rental services have emerged, allowing you to access stylish, designer pieces for a fraction of the retail price. Companies like Rent the Runway, Le Tote, Nuuly, and Fashion Pass offer a range of clothing selections that can be rented for a specific period and then returned, allowing you to keep your wardrobe fresh and on-trend without contributing to fast fashion waste.

UTILIZE SUSTAINABLE MATERIALS:
Look for clothing made from eco-friendly materials like organic cotton, Tencel, hemp, or recycled fibers. These materials have a lower environmental impact than conventional options and can be just as stylish and comfortable.

6 LEVERAGE ONLINE TOOLS FOR SUSTAINABLE SHOPPING:
Numerous apps and browser extensions are available to help you make more sustainable shopping choices. Tools like Good On You, DoneGood, and Project JUST provide ethical and environmental ratings for various fashion brands, making it easier to find items that align with your values.

7 CONNECT WITH LIKE-MINDED INDIVIDUALS:
Join online communities, forums, or social media groups dedicated to sustainable fashion. These platforms allow you to share shopping tips, learn about new brands, and connect with individuals who share your commitment to eco-conscious fashion.

Your Power Dresser wardrobe isn't just any closet; it's a sanctuary — a haven where timeless pieces crafted with integrity reflect your individuality and values.

As you develop this element of power dressing, watch your awareness and confidence grow, alongside a world you're proud to be part of.
—Michele Grant

Maintaining and Organizing Your Wardrobe for Long-Lasting, Sustainable Use

Once you've built a sustainable wardrobe that is both stylish and functional, you will want to put some effort into properly maintaining and organizing it. Proper maintenance can help prolong the life of your garments, reducing the need to buy new items. Here are some tips for maintaining and organizing your wardrobe for long-lasting, mindful use:

1. **FOLLOW CARE INSTRUCTIONS:**
   Each garment has a set of instructions, which should be followed to ensure that the item stays in good condition. Following these instructions will help to keep your clothes looking new for longer.

2. **REPAIR AND REPURPOSE:**
   When a piece of clothing becomes damaged or no longer fits, don't throw it away. Instead, learn how to repair it or repurpose it into something new. This reduces waste and allows you to exercise your creativity to create unique, one-of-a-kind ensembles. Rather than discarding damaged garments or those that no longer fit, consider repairing them or upcycling them into something new. With a little creativity, you can transform a piece of clothing into something entirely different, and thus give it new life.

3. **DEVELOP A STORAGE SYSTEM:**
   One of the keys to maintaining a sustainable wardrobe is taking proper care of your clothing. Develop a storage system that will help you keep your clothes organized and in good condition. Consider investing in high-quality hangers, garment bags, and storage boxes to protect your clothing

from dust and damage. Proper storage is important to maintain the quality of your clothes. Store your clothes in a cool, dry place away from direct sunlight, and hang or fold them properly to avoid wrinkles.

4. **USING ECO-FRIENDLY PRODUCTS:**
Choose eco-friendly laundry detergents and cleaning products, to reduce your carbon footprint. Look for products made with natural ingredients, and avoid harsh chemicals that can harm the environment. You can also support sustainable dry cleaners that use eco-friendly systems and practices to reduce their environmental footprint. Moreover, regular cleaning using eco-friendly detergents that are gentle on the environment will maintain the longevity of your clothes.

5. **CREATE A ROTATING SYSTEM:**
Another effective strategy for maintaining a sustainable wardrobe is implementing a rotating system. Instead of wearing the same items repeatedly, rotate your clothes so that each piece gets equal wear. This prolongs the life of your clothing, allowing you to appreciate each piece more and get the most out of your investment. Also, rotate your wardrobe seasonally, to ensure each piece receives equal use, avoiding wearing certain items too often.

6. **CONSIDER DONATING:**
As you clean out your closet and reorganize for each season, consider donating items you no longer wear. Instead of throwing them away, give them to a charity or organization that accepts clothing donations. This promotes fashion practices that make a difference in multiple ways, by also helping those in need. Many organizations will even provide a tax receipt for your donation, so it's a win-win situation.

By *maintaining* and *organizing* your wardrobe, you'll be able to *enjoy* your clothes for years to come. Increasing their *longevity* reduces the need to constantly buy new items, and donating items contributes to the *upcycling* and *recycling* of them.

Adopting this approach brings a multitude of benefits; it's a commitment to sustainable fashion that can shape a more responsible industry. Instead of being caught in a cycle of endless consumption, we can take pride in a carefully curated collection that supports a more ethical and environmentally conscious way of living. Each piece in our wardrobe thus carries a story, a history, and a future, reflecting a thoughtful approach to fashion that values quality over quantity and purpose over excess.

Balancing Sustainability, Style, and Budget When Building Your Professional Wardrobe

This may sound unheard of, but it is possible to strike the perfect balance between style, sustainability, and budget when building your wardrobe. In fact, you can save money in the long run by investing in quality, durable pieces that will last for years to come. Here are some tips to help you create a wardrobe that supports eco-conscious values, and won't break the bank.

- **THRIFT STORES AND CONSIGNMENT SHOPS** are treasure troves for finding unique, high-quality items at affordable prices. You can often find pieces from high-end brands that are in good condition, at a fraction of the original cost. Moreover, by purchasing secondhand items, you're helping reduce the amount of clothing waste in landfills.

- **RENTAL SUBSCRIPTION SERVICES** are affordable and eco-friendly ways to refresh your wardrobe. Companies like Rent the Runway and Armoire offer monthly subscription services that allow you to rent designer clothes and accessories for a fraction of the cost of buying new ones. This can be particularly useful for special occasions or events where you want to make a statement without breaking the bank.

- **PRE-OWNED ONLINE MARKETPLACES** Depop, Poshmark, and thredUP offer a wide range of pre-owned and vintage clothing options, often at a fraction of the cost of buying new. These platforms allow you to browse and purchase sustainable fashion pieces from the comfort of your home, while supporting small businesses and individuals committed to eco-friendly fashion practices. For those looking for luxury items, online pre-owned luxury retailers like The RealReal and Vestiaire Collective offer authenticated designer clothing, bags, and accessories, at a fraction of the original price. Not only are you saving money, but you're also giving a second life to high-end items that may otherwise have gone to waste.

- **CLOTHING SWAPS** are viable options if you want to expand your sustainable fashion network. Websites like Swap Society and Swap.com allow you to swap clothes with people from all over the world, while promoting sustainable fashion practices and saving money.

But don't forget to pay attention to the style aspect as you progress towards embodying these Power Dresser attributes. After all, fashion is an expression of one's taste and style. The good news is that sustainable fashion is no longer limited to a hippie or bohemian aesthetic. More and more brands offer options catering to a wide range of clothing tastes.

As this arena continues to gain popularity, there is increasing evidence that more consumers are willing to pay a premium for them.

According to a report by Nielsen, 66 percent of global consumers are willing to pay more for *sustainable products*. This demonstrates that sustainability and style are not mutually exclusive, and that investing in these products can also be a *smart long-term decision*.

Versatility is another important factor to consider when balancing sustainability, style, and budget. Choosing pieces that can be styled in multiple ways and worn in various settings will go a long way. This will help you get more wear out of each item and reduce the need to purchase new pieces.

A study by Movinga, involving 18,000 households across 20 countries, found a notable gap between the clothing items people own and those they actually wear. The research revealed that, in countries like Belgium and the United States, a significant portion of wardrobes — up to 88% in Belgium and 82% in the U.S. — had remained unworn over the past year. This underutilization suggests a need for more versatile and compatible clothing choices. By focusing on versatile pieces that can be mixed and matched, consumers can enhance wardrobe utilization and promote sustainable consumption practices, making the most out of each item's value and longevity.

> **Identifying your style preferences will be key to achieving a balanced and sustainable clothing toolbox with a purpose.**
> —Michele Grant

One way to discover your style is to create a moodboard or visual inspiration board that includes images of clothing, colors, and accessories you're drawn to. This can help you identify patterns and themes in your style choices and inform your future purchasing decisions.

Anand Mahindra, the chairman of Mahindra Group, once said, "Sustainability has to be a way of life to be a way of business." By making conscious choices, we can support ethical and sustainable practices while still looking and feeling confident in our professional lives.

In the next chapter, we will delve into the intricacies of navigating dress codes in any professional environment. Dress codes can vary greatly, depending on the industry, company, and event. Understanding these nuances is crucial for presenting oneself professionally and appropriately. We will explore the different dress codes, from casual to formal, and provide tips on building a versatile wardrobe that can be adapted to any situation. Additionally, we'll discuss the importance of nonverbal communication and cultural considerations, equipping you with the knowledge and confidence to excel in any professional setting.

• • •

As we continue on our journey to becoming Power Dressers, let us remember the influence of our choices and the importance of making conscious decisions that reflect our values.

Let's continue to create the world we want to see, one outfit at a time.

chapter 5

NAVIGATING PROFESSIONAL DRESS CODES

Imagine entering a networking event where everyone seems to know what to wear, but you're wondering if your outfit is up to par. The anxiety sets in as you second-guess your choices and wonder if you've made a faux pas. The truth is that dress codes can be a minefield, especially when different industries and events have their own unique standards. In this chapter, I'll provide the tools to help demystify them, whether you're dressing for a business casual office or a formal gala. Get ready to elevate your wardrobe game and show the world what a true Power Dresser is capable of!

Here are the topics we'll cover in this chapter:

- **Decoding the Secrets of Dress Codes**
- **Decoding Dress Codes for Professional Events**
- **Decoding Dress Codes for Specific Professions**

It seems to me that clothes are a form of expression as legitimate as a piece of writing. They are a personal narrative: a story we tell the world about ourselves.

Decoding the Secrets of Dress Codes

Each industry and professional setting has its own unique dress code; you need to understand these nuances in order to avoid the potential embarrassment of dressing inappropriately. Let's unravel the mysteries of the most common dress codes and gain insight into what each entails:

BUSINESS FORMAL:

> This is the pinnacle of professional attire; think boardroom meetings and executive summits, which typically demand a polished and confident presence. For women, this translates to tailored suits in classic colors like black, navy, or gray, or knee-length dresses with clean lines. Skirts and dresses should err on the side of conservative, ensuring appropriate coverage and avoiding overly tight fits. Accessories should complement the overall sophistication, with closed-toe pumps, minimal jewelry, and structured handbags rounding out the ensemble.

BUSINESS PROFESSIONAL:

> This is the everyday powerhouse of corporate dress codes offering, elegance with flexibility. For women, this allows for tailored suits, skirt or trouser suits, blouses or sheath dresses, all in a polished finish. Skirts and dresses should still fall to the knee or below, but bolder colors and subtle patterns are acceptable. Closed-toe pumps with moderate heels remain

the footwear of choice, and jewelry can be slightly more prominent, while maintaining professionalism.

BUSINESS CREATIVE:
This dress code encourages creativity while maintaining a professional appearance. For women, this dress code requires a dress, skirt, or dress pants paired with a blouse or sweater. Patterns and colors can be used sparingly but should not be too bold or bright. Closed-toe pumps or fashionable flats are appropriate, and jewelry can be more expressive.

BUSINESS CASUAL:
This dress code is less formal than business professional; it is becoming increasingly common in the modern workplace. For women, this dress code typically requires slacks or a skirt, a blouse or sweater, and dress shoes or sandals. Skirts or dresses can be knee-length or shorter, but should still be modest. Avoid clothing that is too tight or revealing, and limit jewelry to one or two simple pieces.

SMART CASUAL:
This dress code is a step above business casual; it is appropriate for events like company picnics, corporate retreats, and networking events. For women, this dress code typically requires a dress, skirt, or slacks paired with a blouse or sweater. Patterns and colors can be used more liberally, and fashionable flats, low heels, or loafers are appropriate. Avoid clothing that is too casual, such as denim or sneakers.

CASUAL:
This dress code is the least formal; is typically reserved for everyday events like team-building exercises or casual

Fridays. While relaxed dress codes may vary depending on the workplace, they generally allow for comfortable, casual clothing such as jeans and t-shirts. For women, clothing should still be workplace appropriate, avoiding clothing that is too tight, ripped, or revealing. Sneakers or sandals can be worn, and jewelry should be minimal.

WHITE TIE:

This is the most formal dress code, which is reserved for exclusive events such as state dinners, prestigious award ceremonies, and royal events. For women, white tie requires a full-length formal ball gown, often worn with gloves extending past the elbow, and grand, luxurious formal jewelry, tiaras, and exquisite clutches. Closed-toe high heels and classic pumps in satin or other fine materials are the most appropriate, while delicate, jeweled ankle straps or subtle embellishments can add a touch of opulence.

BLACK TIE AND FORMAL:

Black tie and formal dress codes are synonymous; they are typically worn for events such as weddings, galas, and theater premieres. For women, polished and tailored floor-length gowns, typically made from luxurious fabrics such as silk, satin, or velvet, are ideal. Select formal footwear like high heels, closed-toe pumps, or delicate strappy sandals in colors that complement the gown. Accessories should be tasteful and refined, including stunning jewelry, elegant clutches, and possibly a shawl or wrap.

BLACK TIE OPTIONAL:

This dress code is a step down from formal black tie, falling between formal and semi-formal attire; it is typically seen at upscale parties or dinner banquets. For women, black tie optional can include traditional evening gowns, dressy separates, or a dressy jumpsuit paired with high elegant pumps or embellished kitten heels. Accessories should be formal but not overly extravagant, including fine or statement jewelry and stylish clutches.

CREATIVE BLACK TIE:

This dress code allows for more creativity and expression than traditional black tie. For women, this may mean a colorful gown with beautiful bold prints or unique cuts, such as high-low or asymmetrical gowns. Footwear can be a statement piece with standout designs, colors, or embellishments. Creativity can shine in accessories, with the opportunity to incorporate bold jewelry, distinctive clutches, or artistic hairpieces.

COCKTAIL OR SEMI-FORMAL:

The cocktail and semi-formal dress codes are synonymous. They are dressy but not formal dress codes, typically reserved for evening events. For women, this could mean a knee-length or midi dress, dressy separates, or a dressy jumpsuit paired with dressy heels or flats. Jewelry can be more expressive but still upscale.

UNIFORM ATTIRE:

This dress code is specific to those who wear a uniform for their profession, such as military or law enforcement. For civilian guests attending events where uniform attire is requested, a suit or dressy separates in a neutral color such as black or navy can be appropriate. Footwear should be formal and polished, with conservative heels or flats that complement the outfit. Accessories such as formal

watches and complementary silk scarves can add more style to the look.

RESORT FORMAL:
Commonly seen at tropical destinations, this dress code calls for resort wear such as sundresses, linen pants, and sandals. While it's important to dress appropriately for the destination and event, it's also crucial to maintain a polished, classy appearance. Women can opt for a lightweight, flowing sundress or a blouse paired with a maxi skirt or linen pants. Sandals or wedges can be worn, but it is advisable to avoid flip-flops and athletic shoes.

FESTIVE:
This dress code is often used for holiday parties or other celebratory events where you can opt for a dress or dressy separates with fun accessories. Experiment with fun colors and textures, such as a sequined skirt or metallic top paired with heels. It's important to keep the type of event and audience in mind and not go over the top with accessories or glitter.

GOLF:
Dress codes for golf typically include collared shirts, slacks, Bermuda shorts, and golf shoes. Women may wear sleeveless or collared shirts, skirts, or skorts. However, tank tops, jeans, and athletic shorts or pants are usually not allowed on the golf course. Women can wear golf pants, shorts, or skirts with a collared shirt. It's important to wear appropriate shoes and avoid any clothing that restricts movement or causes discomfort during the swing.

TENNIS:
>Dress codes for tennis often include white skirts or skorts with a white collared or sleeveless shirt and white athletic shoes, often referred to as "tennis whites." However, some tennis clubs may have specific dress codes prohibiting certain clothing types, such as denim or non-athletic shoes. Women can wear white tennis skirts or skorts with a collared or sleeveless shirt. It's important to wear comfortable, supportive athletic shoes and avoid any clothing that restricts movement or causes discomfort during play.

SKI RESORT:
>Ski resorts typically have a dress code that requires appropriate winter sports attire, such as ski jackets, pants, and accessories like gloves and hats. Women can wear insulated ski pants or bibs, and a waterproof coat, along with layers such as a base layer and fleece. It's important to wear appropriate accessories such as gloves, a hat, and goggles, in order to protect yourself against the elements.

GYM/FITNESS/YOGA STUDIOS:
>Some corporate gyms, yoga, or fitness studios may have a dress code that requires appropriate workout attire, such as athletic leggings, shorts, and tops all of which provide comfort and flexibility. Women can opt for athletic leggings, shorts, fitted tank tops, or t-shirts. It is important to choose breathable and moisture-wicking fabrics, to ensure comfort during workouts .

HIKING:
>Dress codes for hiking may vary depending on the level of difficulty and terrain. However, wearing comfortable, breathable clothing and sturdy shoes or boots is important

for safety. Women can opt for moisture-wicking leggings or hiking pants paired with a breathable top and a light jacket. It's also important to bring appropriate gear, such as a hat, sunglasses, and sunscreen to protect against the elements.

SWIMMING POOLS:

Dress codes may include requirements for proper swimwear, such as one-piece bathing suits for women. Some pools may also require caps and goggles, for health and safety reasons. Women can opt for a one-piece swimsuit or a two-piece tankini, along with a cover-up such as a sundress or sarong. It is important to choose swimwear that provides adequate coverage and support while remaining comfortable and stylish.

BOATING/SAILING:

Dress codes for boating and sailing may vary depending on the type of vessel and event. However, it's generally advisable to wear light-colored, breathable clothing that provides protection from the sun and wind for day events. Non-skid or deck shoes are also recommended, to prevent slips and falls on wet surfaces. Women can wear comfortable, casual clothing such as a lightweight shirt or blouse paired with shorts or capris. It's best to avoid any clothing that could get caught on winches, hooks, cleats, or other boating equipment.

EQUESTRIAN:

For equestrian events or settings, the dress code often requires specific attire, such as riding boots, jodhpurs, or breeches, and a riding jacket or vest. Women can opt for equestrian riding pants paired with a collared shirt or sweater. They can also add a stylish touch with a riding jacket

or vest and riding boots. It's important to wear a helmet for safety and to avoid any clothing that could get caught in the saddle or bridle. Choose attire that is comfortable, and that allows for ease of movement while riding.

Level up, Power Dressers! You just graduated from Fashion 101. This intel is your golden ticket to putting your best foot forward, commanding attention like a boss, and achieving your dreams.

> **Grab your power suit and strut your stuff, because the world's your catwalk, and you're about to walk it like you own it!**
> —Michele Grant

Decoding Dress Codes for Professional Events

Understanding dress codes for different professional events is crucial for projecting a confident and professional image. While dress codes for various events can vary widely, it's important to understand the general guidelines, so you can feel confident in your attire and avoid any potential faux pas. Let's explore some of the most common professional events and their corresponding dress codes.

CONFERENCES AND TRADE SHOWS:

These events often have an atmosphere of industry leadership and business ingenuity that requires attendees to dress accordingly. The dress code may vary depending on the industry and specific event, but it's generally recommended to dress in business professional or business casual attire. Women can opt for a tailored suit, dress, or dress pants with a blouse while ensuring their accessories are eloquent and shoes are polished.

NETWORKING EVENTS:

These events provide opportunities to connect with professionals in your industry and make lasting connections. The dress code for these events can range from business professional to business casual, depending on the setting and purpose. Women can choose a conservative dress, skirt, or pants with a blouse or a tailored pantsuit, with stylish yet comfortable shoes. Adding a statement accessory or blazer can also elevate the outfit.

GALAS AND FUNDRAISERS:

These events are elegant affairs that often require black tie or black tie optional attire. Women can select a floor-length gown or a sophisticated cocktail dress, with attention to the event's theme and formality. Complementary accessories and tasteful jewelry can enhance the overall look, exuding confidence and grace.

AWARD CEREMONIES:

These are events where industry professionals are recognized or celebrated with awards, with local, national, or international viewership. Depending on the occasion, dress codes can fall within a wide range, from white tie to

cocktail. Paying attention to the event's theme, venue, and specific dress code instructions will be a necessary element for selecting the appropriate attire. Once the dress code instructions are established, women can choose options within them, such as a formal evening gown or a chic cocktail dress that reflects their individual taste.

COMPANY PARTIES:

These events can vary in dress code, from casual to semi-formal. It's important to understand the nature of the event and any guidelines provided by the company. For casual company parties, women can opt for stylish, comfortable outfits such as dressy jeans or trousers paired with a blouse or trendy top. A cocktail dress or a chic jumpsuit can be appropriate choices for semi-formal company parties. Accessorize with statement jewelry and heels to elevate the look.

JOB INTERVIEWS:

These are pivotal moments in your career journey, and dressing appropriately is crucial to making a positive impression. Research the company culture and opt for business professional attire, such as a well-fitted suit in a conservative color like navy, black, or gray. Pair the suit with a tailored blouse, closed-toe pumps, and minimal yet polished accessories. Aim for a sophisticated and polished appearance that conveys your leadership and confidence.

INDUSTRY CONFERENCES:

These events bring professionals together for educational sessions, panel discussions, and networking opportunities. The dress code for industry conferences can vary depending on the specific field and the conference's focus. Women should aim for a business professional and polished look, choosing attire that aligns with the overall tone of the event. A tailored suit, dress, or dress pants with a blouse can be suitable options. Consider incorporating subtle elements that reflect your industry or individual taste, such as a statement accessory or a pop of color.

PROFESSIONAL PANEL DISCUSSIONS:

These events gather industry experts to share insights and discuss relevant topics. As a panelist, it's important to dress in a manner that conveys your expertise and experience, with a touch of your personality. Use the business professional or business creative dress codes and go for a tailored dress or a skirt suit paired with a blouse or a sophisticated top. Choose colors and patterns that are visually appealing, but not distracting. Wear comfortable yet stylish shoes, as you may be on your feet during the discussion. Pay attention to grooming and overall presentation in order to exude confidence and credibility.

BUSINESS LUNCHEONS:

These events are formal or semi-formal daytime events where professionals gather for networking and discussions. The dress code can range from business professional to business casual. Women can wear tailored pantsuits, dresses, or skirt and blouse combinations, paired with polished accessories.

VIP RECEPTIONS:

These exclusive events require sophisticated and upscale attire. The dress code can range from cocktail attire to black tie. Choose from elegant cocktail dresses, floor-length gowns, or tailored separates paired with high-end accessories.

PRODUCT LAUNCHES:
These are exciting events where new products or services are introduced to the market. Navigate the dress code spectrum based on the brand's vibe and image. Channel a sleek approach to the business professional or business creative dress codes and opt for stylish and contemporary outfits that reflect the brand's aesthetics, while still maintaining a first-rate appearance.

CORPORATE RETREATS:
These events often involve a mix of work and leisure activities. Depending on the location and agenda, the dress code can range from casual to resort casual. Wear comfortable yet stylish outfits like casual dresses, skirts, or pants paired with breezy tops and comfortable shoes.

MEDIA INTERVIEWS:
These events call for a polished and camera-friendly appearance. The dress code can vary from business professional to business creative, depending on the nature of the interview and the media outlet. It's important to dress smart, opting for a tailored outfit in solid colors and minimal patterns. Consider a structured blazer or dress with appropriate makeup and accessories that enhance your presence on camera.

PROFESSIONAL DEVELOPMENT WORKSHOPS:
These are educational events, where learning and networking take place. The dress code is usually business casual, allowing for a more relaxed yet office-appropriate look. Wear slacks or a skirt with a blouse paired with comfortable yet stylish shoes.

CORPORATE DINNERS:
> The dress codes for these events can vary from business formal to smart casual, depending on the event and venue. Choose elegant, sophisticated tailored suits or conservative dresses with closed-toe pumps or traditional heels. Accessories should be slightly more expressive while still maintaining a refined look.

ART GALLERY OPENINGS:
> These events are often sophisticated and stylish. The dress code can vary, but it is typically on the dressier side of smart casual or business casual. A chic dress or tailored pantsuit paired with statement accessories would be appropriate.

FASHION INDUSTRY EVENTS:
> Events such as fashion shows, runway reveals, or industry parties require fashionable and on-trend attire. Use the business creative dress code to curate stylish outfits that reflect the latest fashion trends. A well-constructed dress, tailored separates, or a fashion-forward jumpsuit in bolder colors and subtle patterns that work well paired with statement accessories.

CLIENT MEETINGS:
> These sessions call for a neat and well-put-together appearance to instill confidence and trust. Use the business professional or business casual dress codes and opt for a tailored dress or skirt with a blouse, classic heels, and minimalistic accessories.

PROFESSIONAL ASSOCIATION EVENTS:
> These events are important networking opportunities for industry leaders and top talent. Depending on the industry

and association, the dress code can vary from business professional to business casual. Choosing a tailored suit or dress with conservative yet stylish accessories would be a suitable choice.

Your clothes are the billboard, announce yourself.
–G.K. Chesterton

In the professional arena, choosing the right attire becomes an art form, an unspoken language that speaks volumes about your confidence and competence. Forget rigid rules and boring boilerplates — understanding dress codes will empower you to curate a wardrobe that's uniquely you. When you dress with intention, you not only navigate professional settings with ease, but you also exude a presence that whispers, "I belong here, and I mean business."

The key to dressing for different professional events is to strike a balance between career aspirations, individuality, and appropriateness for the specific occasion. Imparting an air of self-assurance and refinement requires familiarity with the dress requirements for different types of business occasions. Tailoring your attire to each event will show your corporate awareness and dedication to presenting your best self.

If you find yourself uncertain about the *dress code* for a particular event, feel free to reach out for clarification. The event organizer or your contacts within the *industry* can provide *valuable insights* to ensure you're dressed appropriately.

If all else fails, don't fret! You can try a helpful trick: look up past event photos online. Many companies and organizations share pictures from past events on their websites or social media platforms. By taking a quick search, you can get a glimpse of how attendees dressed and gain valuable insights into the expected dress code. Pay attention to the overall aesthetic and level of formality in the photos, and use them as a reference point to guide your outfit selection. So, take advantage of the online resources available and let them guide you towards a perfectly curated and appropriate ensemble.

As you waltz through your calendar of events, each occasion becomes a stage for your professional brand's grand entrance. By mastering the art of dressing appropriately for each situation, you're taking a major step towards becoming the Power Dressers you've all aspired to be. So, shed the mundane, and embrace the sartorial spotlight. In this professional performance, every Power Dresser is a standing ovation waiting to happen. Own the stage. Own your style. Own your success.

Decoding Dress Codes for Specific Professions

Forging a polished image starts with understanding the unspoken language of attire. Each industry has its own set of expectations and conventions for attire, and mastering the art of code-cracking elegance can be the key to building credibility and commanding respect. Let's delve into the nuances of interpreting dress standards across various professions, with actionable tips for navigating the workplace with awareness and poise.

LEGAL PROFESSION:
In the esteemed halls of the legal world, a business professional image reigns supreme. Women command respect in tailored suits, skirts, or pantsuits in classic colors, exuding authority with knee-length or longer hemlines and polished blouses. Minimal, understated accessories and closed-toe pumps complete the picture of dignified deportment.

CREATIVE INDUSTRIES:
Unleash your artistic flair within the boundaries of the business creative dress code. Advertising, fashion, and design fields welcome unique expression, but maintain professionalism. Experiment with trendy pieces, patterns, and colors while avoiding anything overly casual or revealing. Stylish accessories, bold combinations, and trendy footwear can add your signature touch.

HEALTHCARE AND MEDICAL FIELDS:
Hygiene and trust take center stage in healthcare. Doctors, nurses, and medical professionals adhere to scrubs protocol, following guidelines set by their facility. Administrative staff in medical offices may lean towards business casual, prioritizing comfort and practicality within the workplace.

FINANCIAL SERVICES:
Confidence is key in the financial world. Opt for business professional attire with tailored suits, skirts, or pantsuits in conservative colors. Understated accessories and polished, closed-toe footwear reflect the industry's emphasis on trust and competence.

TECHNOLOGY AND STARTUPS:

Innovation thrives in a more relaxed realm. While casual attire like jeans and sneakers may be acceptable, consider the context, your aspirations, and typical business interactions. For client meetings or formal gatherings, elevate your game to business casual or even business professional, for impactful appearances.

EDUCATION:

The education sector often follows a business casual or smart casual dress code. For women, this can include skirts, slacks, or dresses paired with blouses or tops. Adhere to the specific guidelines set by your educational institution, while exhibiting your style within the professional boundaries.

CORPORATE EXECUTIVES:

Lead with power and sophistication. As a corporate executive, business professional attire is your armor. Tailored suits in neutral or dark colors paired with high-quality blouses or shirts set the tone. Impeccable fit, quality materials, and curated accessories contribute to an aura of leadership and command respect.

HOSPITALITY AND SERVICE INDUSTRY:

In the world of hospitality, presentation is key. For front-of-house staff, uniforms that define the establishment's image may be provided. Ensure yours is clean, well-fitted, and reflects the brand's culture. Managerial or administrative roles may have more flexibility, allowing for business casual or smart casual attire. Focus on impeccable yet comfortable outfits that complement the overall vibe of the establishment.

GOVERNMENT AND PUBLIC SECTOR:

The government and public sector often use the business formal dress code to convey their official standing and respect for the position. Tailored suits, dresses, or skirt suits in conservative colors are typically expected. Minimalistic accessories, closed-toe shoes, and modest hemlines are most appropriate, as they demonstrate a commitment to public service.

ENGINEERING AND TECHNICAL FIELDS:

The dress code in engineering and technical fields tends to lean towards business casual or casual attire, especially in more relaxed work environments. Opt for well-fitted pants or skirts paired with collared shirts, blouses, or sweaters. While there may be more flexibility in terms of attire, maintaining a neat and well-put-together appearance is still the go-to standard.

SALES AND CLIENT-FACING ROLES:

Building trust is essential in client-facing roles. Dress codes can range from business casual to business professional depending on the industry and company culture. Aim for well-tailored suits, dresses, or separates in classic colors, and pay attention to grooming and accessories, in order to convey a trustworthy and competent image.

By deciphering the dress code of your domain, you *unlock* a *powerful tool* for *success.* Whether commanding respect in the tailored suits of the legal realm, expressing your creativity in the vibrant world of advertising, or navigating the *dynamic landscape* of tech in polished *comfort*, your attire becomes a *silent language* of *competence* and *confidence.*

> **Own your space, cultivate your unique style, and watch your presence blossom.**
> —Michele Grant

• • •

The journey deepens in the next chapter, in which we embark on an exploration of nonverbal communication and cultural nuances in professional attire. Embrace this ongoing evolution, and watch your Power Dresser persona flourish.

chapter 6

LEARNING THE NONVERBAL AND CULTURAL LANGUAGES OF PROFESSIONAL ATTIRE

> **What you wear is how you present yourself to the world, especially today, when human contacts are so quick. Fashion is instant language.**
> –Miuccia Prada

Imagine entering a room, whether physically or virtually, surrounded by veterans from diverse backgrounds and cultural contexts. As you observe the attendees, you realize that their attire speaks volumes about their awareness, values, and respect for the occasion.

Understanding the intricacies of nonverbal communication, cultural considerations, and digital etiquette in professional attire is paramount to establishing positive and memorable connections in any setting.

In this chapter, we will explore the following topics:

- **Understanding the impact of nonverbal communication on professional dress**
- **Navigating cultural considerations in professional dress codes**
- **Adapting to digital etiquette, for professional attire in virtual settings**

Power dressing will always be interpreted in the light of cultural sensitivity, digital etiquette, and nonverbal communication. Each topic will furnish you with knowledge and actionable approaches with which to bolster your powerhouse image in the real world as well as the digital realm. A strong approach to power dressing in the digital environment is waiting for you when you unlock these sartorial gems.

Understanding the Impact of Nonverbal Communication on Professional Dress

In the world of power dressing, it's not just about the clothes we wear — it's also about the nonverbal cues we communicate through our appearance. Our attire and grooming choices send powerful messages to others, shaping their perceptions of our adeptness, eloquence, and attention to detail. In this section, we will explore the impact of nonverbal communication on professional dress and delve into the question of how to make intentional choices.

> **“**
> **The way we look is frequently the first thing that people notice about us, and first impressions are important.**
> **—Michele Grant**
> **”**

According to studies, people have already formulated an opinion about someone within the first few seconds of meeting them, based on what they're wearing. That is why it is so important to be aware of the nonverbal cues that our clothes, personal hygiene, and body language provide.

One aspect of nonverbal communication is our attire's level of formality. Dressing appropriately for a professional setting demonstrates respect for the environment and conveys the message that we take our work seriously. Consider the industry, company culture, and specific context when choosing our outfits. For example, a conservative business suit may suit a formal corporate setting. In contrast, business casual attire with a touch of creativity may be more appropriate for a creative industry.

Grooming is just as important as clothing to nonverbal communication. A high-caliber look can be achieved with well-groomed hair, proper makeup, and well-maintained nails. Making an effort to look good demonstrates that we are detail-oriented and proud of the work we do.

Body language is another vital element of nonverbal communication. How we carry ourselves, our posture, and our gestures all contribute to how we appear and our overall presence. Standing tall, maintaining eye contact, and offering a firm handshake demonstrate a confident leader. Conversely, slouching, avoiding eye contact, or fidgeting can undermine our assertiveness and make us appear less competent.

Considering nonverbal communication in business attire requires an understanding of cultural conventions and context. When it comes to personal hygiene, dress code, and nonverbal cues, different cultures may have different expectations. Being respectful and considerate of these cultural factors goes a long way in creating a welcoming workplace for people of all backgrounds.

Nonverbal cues can convey a lot, ***beyond*** the ***basics*** of how we look. Being aware of how nonverbal cues will affect the way we ***present ourselves*** in a professional setting; this will allow us to make ***deliberate decisions*** that are in line with our ***principles*** and ***objectives***.

Improving the way others see us can be as simple as dressing the part, keeping our hair and nails trimmed properly, and paying attention to our body language. No matter how much of a minimalist or daring approach we want to take, it is critical to adapt our Power Dresser clothing toolbox to meet the standards of the workplace.

Consider the story of Sarah, a young professional eager to make her mark in the corporate world. She paid meticulous attention to her attire, always dressing in tailored suits and stylish accessories. However, despite her impeccable appearance, she needed help to make meaningful connections with colleagues and clients. It wasn't until she attended a workshop on nonverbal communication that she realized her body language conveyed a sense of aloofness and detachment. Sarah learned to make subtle adjustments, such as maintaining open and approachable body language, actively listening, and engaging in genuine conversations. These changes transformed her business interactions, and she began to build authentic connections that propelled her career forward.

You can improve your skills in projecting an attractive and convincing leadership persona by integrating the following tips into your knowledge of nonverbal cues and their effects on business attire. Bear in mind that your demeanor and nonverbal communication with people are equally as important as the clothes you wear. Being deliberate in your decision-making and consistently honing your nonverbal communication abilities crafts a powerful presence that resonates long after introductions.

1. DRESS APPROPRIATELY FOR THE OCCASION:
Understand the dress code for different professional settings and events, as discussed earlier. By adhering to the expected level of formality, you demonstrate respect for the environment and show that you take your expertise and trajectory seriously.

2. PAY ATTENTION TO GROOMING:
Take care of your appearance by maintaining well-groomed hair, appropriate makeup, and neat nails. These small details can make a big difference to how others perceive you and contribute to a polished look.

3. BE CULTURALLY SENSITIVE:
In today's interconnected world, it is crucial to be aware of and respectful of different cultural practices. Invest some effort into learning the norms and customs of the workplaces where you will be working. Possessing this knowledge will equip you to thrive in diverse environments and cultivate strong relationships with clients and coworkers hailing from all walks of life.

4. DRESS FOR YOUR ROLE:
Consider the expectations and norms of your specific role and specialty. Dressing in a way that aligns with, or even exceeds the expectations of your position can help establish credibility and authority. Take cues from respected individuals in your field and aim to project a professional image that reflects your expertise and the next step you want to take in your career.

5 PAY ATTENTION TO YOUR POSTURE:
Be mindful of your body language and posture. Stand tall with your shoulders back and offer a firm handshake. Avoid slouching, hunching, or fidgeting, as these behaviors can undermine your assertiveness. These simple adjustments can instantly enhance your overall presence.

6 MIND YOUR FACIAL EXPRESSIONS:
Your face is a powerful tool for nonverbal communication. Be mindful of your facial expressions, as they can convey a range of emotions and attitudes. Maintain a pleasant and approachable expression, and be aware of any unintentional frowns, scowls, or excessive laughing that may undermine your professional demeanor.

7 USE APPROPRIATE HAND GESTURES:
Hand gestures can enhance your verbal communication and emphasize your points. However, be mindful of using gestures that are too exaggerated or distracting. Aim for natural and purposeful hand movements that complement your words.

8 MAINTAIN EYE CONTACT:
Making eye contact is an important way to connect and build trust. Make an effort to keep eye contact with the person you are talking to, to communicate that you are paying attention and are interested in the conversation.

9 PRACTICE ACTIVE LISTENING:
Nonverbal communication is not just about how you present yourself; it's also about how you interpret and respond to others. Practice active listening by nodding, maintaining an

open body posture, and using appropriate facial expressions to show that you are engaged and attentive.

10. PAY ATTENTION TO YOUR TONE OF VOICE:
Your tone can significantly influence how your message is received. Aim for a confident and assertive tone without sounding arrogant or overly aggressive. Speak clearly and at an appropriate volume, in order to ensure your words are effectively conveyed.

11. BE AWARE OF PERSONAL SPACE:
Respect personal boundaries and be mindful of the appropriate distance to maintain during professional interactions. Invading someone's personal space can make them uncomfortable, while keeping too much distance can create a disconnection. Adapt your proximity based on the cultural norms and comfort levels of those around you.

12. SMILE GENUINELY:
A warm, genuine smile can instantly create a good impression and foster a welcoming atmosphere. Smiling naturally and authentically is always better than a forced or insincere smile that can come across as inauthentic.

> **"**
> Power Dressers, bear
> in mind that all aspects
> of your presentation
> say a lot about your
> decorum and drive.
> —Michele Grant
> **"**

One of the most effective ways to control how others see you in the business world is to master the art of nonverbal communication. Once you do that, you're well on your way.

Use body language to your advantage, work on your brand, and walk into the workplace with ease and self-assurance. Being a Power Dresser isn't just about what you wear; it's also about growing as a person in your specialty and your career, in order to reach your full potential.

Navigating Cultural Considerations in Professional Dress Codes

It is important to understand and respect ethnic differences when it comes to dress rules. Keeping in mind that different cultures have different rules and ideas about what people should wear to work shows that you value difference, and you know that it helps people work together in international settings. To help you figure out how to follow the cultural rules for business attire, let's look at some important things to remember:

1. **RESEARCH AND FAMILIARIZE YOURSELF:**
   Before engaging with business professionals from different cultural backgrounds, take the time to research and familiarize yourself with their cultural norms and customs regarding dress. Understanding the cultural context will help you make informed choices and avoid unintentional missteps.

2. **BE AWARE OF MODESTY REQUIREMENTS:**
   The standards of modesty can differ greatly from culture to culture. Certain cultures place a greater emphasis on modest clothing, mandating that women cover their arms,

legs, and shoulders. Some cultures, however, have more lenient standards. It's important to honor these cultural norms and modify your wardrobe appropriately.

3 CONSIDER RELIGIOUS PRACTICES:
Religion can play a role in shaping dress codes as well. Some religions have specific guidelines for modesty and clothing choices. For example, in Islamic culture, women may wear hijabs or headscarves, while Sikh men may wear turbans. Respect religious practices by being aware of, and sensitive to, these requirements.

4 PAY ATTENTION TO COLOR SYMBOLISM:
Colors can hold different symbolic meanings across cultures. For instance, white is associated with mourning in some Eastern cultures, while red is considered auspicious in many Asian cultures. Be mindful of color symbolism to ensure your choices align with cultural norms and avoid unintended offense.

5 ADAPT TO LOCAL CUSTOMS:
When working or attending events in different countries or regions, it's crucial to embrace the local customs and traditions with a touch of charm and cleverness. Take note of how the local professionals dress and adjust your attire accordingly. If you're unsure, it's always a good idea to play it safe and dress more conservatively, until you get a better grasp of the cultural norms.

6 SEEK GUIDANCE AND ASK QUESTIONS:
Feel free to seek guidance if you need clarification on the cultural expectations regarding business dressing. Contact colleagues, mentors, or cultural advisors who can provide

insights and advice. You show respect and a genuine commitment to understanding cultural diversity by asking questions and demonstrating your willingness to learn.

7. AVOID CULTURAL APPROPRIATION:
Cultural appropriation refers to adopting or imitating elements of another culture inappropriately or without understanding their significance. It's important to avoid appropriating cultural attire or symbols without proper understanding and respect. Appreciate cultural diversity but do so with sensitivity and appreciation rather than imitation.

8. OBSERVE CULTURAL COLOR ASSOCIATIONS:
When you are dressing for international business meetings or events, you should always consider the cultural meaning of colors in the nation you are visiting. With this knowledge, you'll be able to choose your clothing with confidence and make sure it's conveying the correct message.

9. EMBRACE INCLUSIVE ATTIRE:
In today's globalized workplaces, organizations are increasingly embracing inclusive dress codes that accommodate diverse cultural backgrounds. Encourage dialogue within your workplace to establish dress code policies that respect and celebrate cultural diversity, fostering a more inclusive and welcoming environment for everyone.

10. MAINTAIN PROFESSIONALISM:
Taking ethnic factors into account is important, but it's also important to approach this responsibly. Make sure that your clothing is still appropriate for a business setting and that it

fits with what the industry or group expects, even if you are meeting cultural norms.

11. CULTIVATE OPEN-MINDEDNESS AND RESPECT:
Above all, approach cultural considerations with an open mind and a genuine respect for diversity. Seek opportunities to learn from different cultures and be open to incorporating new perspectives into your business approach. By cultivating a mindset of respect and inclusivity, you will contribute to a harmonious and culturally aware work atmosphere.

12. SEEK GUIDANCE FROM LOCAL RESOURCES:
When working or attending events in a different country or culture, consult local resources, so that you understand the specific cultural norms and standards. Local cultural centers, online forums, or even local businesspeople can provide valuable insights into appropriate attire.

13. PAY ATTENTION TO BODY LANGUAGE AND GESTURES:
In addition to attire, body language and gestures can vary across cultures. Be mindful of cultural differences in handshakes, greetings, and other nonverbal communication cues. Observing and adapting to local customs will help you build rapport and avoid misunderstandings.

14. INFUSE CULTURAL DIVERSITY INTO YOUR WARDROBE:
Celebrate cultural diversity by incorporating elements from different cultures into your professional wardrobe. This could be through the use of traditional patterns, accessories, or colors that reflect the richness of different cultural backgrounds. However, ensure that you do so respectfully, and without appropriating sacred or religious symbols.

15. LEAD BY EXAMPLE:

As a professional, you can lead by example when embracing cultural considerations. By showcasing respect for cultural diversity through your attire and behavior, you will inspire others to do the same. Your actions can help shape a workplace culture that values and appreciates different cultural backgrounds.

Remember, cultural considerations reflect your awareness, respect, and ability to navigate diverse environments. By embracing cultural diversity and adapting your approach accordingly, you can enhance your professional relationships and contribute to a more inclusive and harmonious work environment.

Adapting to Digital Etiquette for Professional Attire in Virtual Settings

> **Power Dressers, your professional image extends beyond physical encounters and into the virtual realm.**
> —Michele Grant

In an era where remote work and digital interactions have become the norm, adapting to digital etiquette is essential to maintaining credibility and building rapport. This section will help you navigate the nuances of virtual settings, ensuring that you project first-rate professionalism, regardless of the digital platform.

1 DRESS THE PART:
Just because you work from home doesn't mean you should neglect your attire. Dressing professionally for virtual interactions can help create a focused and productive mindset. Opt for clothing that aligns with your style and the expectations of your industry. A study published in the *Journal of Experimental Social Psychology* by Slepian, Ferber, Gold, and Rutchick in 2015, demonstrates the fact that formal attire can significantly enhance abstract thinking and foster a greater sense of power. By dressing professionally, you ace this new arena, and signal to others that you take your work seriously.

2 CONSIDER COLOR CHOICES:
Understand how color psychology can be your secret weapon in virtual meetings! Strengthen your presence on camera and use certain hues to project an aura that stands out as much as your ideas do. Consider lighting and tone as well, and refrain from shades of red or yellow that lend an unintended sallowness. Shades of blue and gray project an aura of competence and trustworthiness. Opt for these hues or other muted tones while avoiding excessively bright or distracting patterns that can look blurry on camera.

3 DRESS FOR THE CONTEXT:
Different virtual settings may have varying expectations for attire. While some meetings may require a more formal look, others may allow business casual attire. Research the company culture and expectations beforehand, and tailor your clothing accordingly. Dressing in context

demonstrates respect for the occasion and the people you are engaging with.

4. **EXPERIMENT WITH DIFFERENT APPROACHES:**
Virtual interactions unlock a playground for exploring beyond your physical wardrobe! Embrace this opportunity, but with a strategic eye. Consider how lighting and camera angles can affect fabric textures and necklines. Play with different silhouettes, colors, and accessories, seeking what flatters your image and resonates with your brand. By mastering the nuances of the virtual realm, you'll craft a distinct and memorable dynamic presence that projects success in the digital space.

5. **MIND THE NECKLINE:**
The camera angle in virtual meetings often focuses on your upper body, making the neckline of your attire the priority. Opt for necklines that flatter your face shape. Higher necklines are generally perceived as more formal and authoritative. In comparison, lower necklines may project a more casual or relaxed image. Your video presence hangs on that fine balance between professional polish and personalized distinction. Anchor authority at the first glance, then redirect the attention to your leadership.

6. **PAY ATTENTION TO FABRICS:**
The texture and quality of fabrics can boost your overall appearance in virtual settings. Some materials, such as silk or satin, may create glare or appear differently on camera, compared to real life. Consider opting for fabrics with a matte finish, as they tend to translate well in digital environments. Experiment with different fabrics to find those that look top-notch on camera.

7. OPTIMIZE YOUR ACCESSORIES:
While it's important to keep accessories subtle, and not overpowering, strategically chosen standout pieces can enhance your presence in virtual settings. Consider wearing statement earrings or a tasteful necklace that draws attention to your face without being a distraction. These accessories can add a touch of tasteful sophistication.

8. ATTENTION TO FIT:
The fit of your clothing is crucial, even in a virtual environment. Ill-fitting attire can create distractions and detract from your professionalism. Choose garments that fit well and flatter your body shape. Take the time to adjust your camera angle and review your appearance before virtual meetings, to ensure everything looks polished and put together.

9. EMBRACE PROFESSIONAL PRINTS:
While solid colors are generally recommended for virtual settings, prints can add visual interest to your attire. Opt for subtle and sophisticated patterns, such as pinstripes or small geometric designs, that do not distract from your overall presence. Prints can add a creative flair, while maintaining a professional aesthetic.

10. CONSIDER PROPORTIONS:
Bear in mind that the camera's perspective affects how your outfit appears on screen. Opt for clothing that fits well and flatters your figure. Avoid overly loose or baggy attire that may appear sloppy or unprofessional. Similarly, avoid excessively tight clothing that may be uncomfortable or create distractions. Choose clothing with appropriate proportions that present you in the best light during your virtual engagements.

> **Brace yourselves, Power Dressers, because the adventure is far from over!**
> —Michele Grant

Now is the moment to take this to the next level. Prepare to compose a visual symphony in which precision is paramount, and every detail will be a catalyst to your business excellence.

• • •

Join me in the next chapter as we embark on a stylish adventure and unlock the secrets to creating a stellar, polished persona that can supercharge your presence. We will explore the art of enhancing your professional image through accessories, footwear, and grooming. These elements will serve as the finishing touches that complete your ensemble with confidence and finesse.

chapter 7

ENHANCING YOUR STYLE WITH ACCESSORIES, FOOTWEAR, AND GROOMING

Grooming, shoes, and accessories are key components that can elevate your business aesthetic. In this chapter, we'll look at how to use these fundamental elements to improve your style.

Here are the topics we'll cover:

- **Accentuating your professional style with jewelry and accessories**
- **Choosing footwear and handbags that define your professional persona**
- **Polishing your professional image with hair, nails, skincare, and makeup**

Let's discover a treasure trove of insights and practical tips covering the allure of accessories, the unwavering confidence that can come from the perfect footwear, and the finesse of grooming.

Accentuating Your Professional Style with Jewelry and Accessories

> **I've always believed that you should never underestimate the power of a great accessory.**
> –Tory Burch

Accessories have the remarkable ability to add that final touch of flair and individuality to your ensemble. They play a vital role in accentuating your brand and projecting confidence. They act as punctuation marks that elevate your outfit and make a statement without saying a word.

When it comes to jewelry and accessories, the options are endless. Each piece can convey a different vibe and reflect your unique personality, from delicate necklaces to statement earrings. As you select your accessories, consider mixing metals, experimenting with layering, or opting for timeless classics that stand the test of time. Remember, it's not about wearing all the accessories at once, but about choosing the right ones that complement your outfit and highlight your best features.

Let's explore some key considerations when it comes to selecting jewelry and accessories:

1. **EMBRACE THE POWER OF SIMPLICITY:**
   In professional attire, simplicity often reigns supreme. Opt for elegant and understated pieces that complement your outfit without overwhelming it. Minimalist necklaces, delicate bracelets, and timeless stud earrings can add a touch of sophistication to your ensemble, without stealing the spotlight.

2. **CONSIDER THE OCCASION:**
   Different business settings and events call for different levels of formality in this area too. Be mindful of the occasion and choose jewelry and accessories that align with its tone. For a formal business meeting, opt for classic pieces that exude high-caliber elegance. In a more creative or casual setting, you can experiment with bolder or more eclectic choices.

3. **QUALITY OVER QUANTITY:**
   Investing in quality jewelry and accessories ensures longevity and enhances your overall image. Opt for well-crafted pieces made from high-quality materials such as sterling silver, gold, or fine gemstones. These pieces will withstand the test of time and exude a sense of refinement and attention to detail.

4. **BALANCE IS KEY:**
   When accessorizing, strike a harmonious balance between your jewelry and outfit. If you're wearing a statement necklace, pair it with subtler earrings, or vice versa. Avoid overwhelming your ensemble with too many bold pieces that

will be competing for attention. Remember, your jewelry should enhance your overall look, not overpower it.

5. **SHOWCASE YOUR CREATIVITY:**
   Jewelry and accessories provide a unique opportunity to showcase your individuality and creativity. Experiment with different materials, textures, and colors to find pieces that resonate with your aesthetic. Whether you prefer contemporary designs, vintage-inspired pieces, or bohemian accents, let your jewelry be an expression of your authentic self.

6. **CONSIDER THE DETAILS:**
   Pay attention to the finer details when selecting jewelry and accessories. Consider how they complement your skin tone, hair color, and facial features. You should also take into account any special considerations, such as allergies or sensitivities to certain materials.

Aside from the aforementioned factors, let's delve into various types of jewelry that can greatly enhance your professional style:

1. **TIMELESS PEARLS:**
   Pearls have long been associated with elegance and sophistication. Whether in the form of a classic strand necklace, stud earrings, or a delicate bracelet, pearls can add a touch of refinement to your ensembles. Opt for freshwater or cultured pearls in neutral tones such as white, cream, or blush, as they can effortlessly complement a wide range of outfits.

2 STATEMENT RINGS:

A well-chosen statement ring can become a conversation starter and an expression of your style. Look for rings with unique designs, eye-catching gemstones, or intricate detailing. A statement ring can be worn on its own to create a focal point, or paired with more delicate rings for a layered effect.

3 ELEGANT WATCHES:

A quality, stylish watch is a practical accessory and a symbol of class and punctuality. Choose a watch with a timeless design, such as a sleek stainless steel or leather strap with a minimalist dial. Consider both form and function, ensuring the watch complements your wrist size and fits comfortably.

4 VERSATILE HOOP EARRINGS:

Hoop earrings are universal classics that can effortlessly transition from day to night and from casual to formal settings. Opt for small to medium-sized hoops in gold or silver, as they strike a balance between understated elegance and eye-catching appeal. Choose a thickness that complements your facial features and hairstyle.

5 DELICATE CHAINS AND PENDANTS:

Delicate chains with meaningful pendants can be a beautiful way to personalize your outfits. Choose pendants that resonate with your values or represent something significant to you. It could be a symbol of strength, a meaningful word, or a representation of a cherished memory. Layering different chain lengths and pendants can create a unique and personalized look.

In addition to jewelry, there are other accessories that can be useful adornments to any ensemble. Consider the following guidelines when incorporating different types of accessories into your wardrobe:

> **Given the choice, I would spend my money on accessories.**
> **–Iris Apfel**

1. **CHIC SCARVES:**
   Scarves are versatile accessories that can add a touch of elegance and sophistication to your outfit. Opt for silk or lightweight fabric scarves with classic patterns or solid colors. Experiment with different ways of wearing them, such as draping them loosely around your neck, tying them in a stylish knot, or using them as a headscarf. Scarves can instantly elevate a simple blouse or dress and provide a polished finishing touch.

2. **CLASSIC NECKTIE SCARVES:**
   Necktie scarves are go-to accessories for professional settings, particularly for formal or business environments. Choose high-quality silk necktie scarves in classic colors and patterns like stripes, dots, or solids. Pay attention to the width of the tie, ensuring it complements the lapel width of your blazer or suit jacket. Learn how to tie different knots, such as the Windsor, the half-Windsor, or the four-in-hand, to add variety and sophistication to your looks.

3 STYLISH HEADBANDS:
Headbands are stylish, yet practical for keeping your hair in place. Opt for headbands in sleek and sophisticated designs, such as slim bands in neutral colors or those embellished with understated details like pearls or crystals. Headbands can add a touch of femininity and elegance to your hairstyle, whether you wear your hair up or down.

4 BELTED ACCESSORIES:
Belts are functional accessories that can also do a lot for your look. Choose belts that are of high quality, and that complement the color and feel of your outfits. A well-fitted belt can define your waist and add a polished touch to dresses, blouses, and tailored pants. Experiment with different widths and buckles to suit the occasion.

5 STATEMENT BROOCHES:
Brooches are versatile accessories that can instantly add a touch of individuality when pinned on blazers, cardigans, or even scarves. Look for brooches in unique designs, such as floral motifs, geometric shapes, or vintage-inspired pieces. To personalize your outfit further, consider brooches that have a special meaning or that reflect your interests.

So, take inspiration from the wise words of Iris Apfel and embrace accessories as the exclamation point in your fashion statement.

With the right *jewelry, scarves, neckties*, and *headbands*, you can confidently showcase your *personality* and *spark conversations*.

Choosing Footwear and Handbags That Define Your Professional Persona

Don't underestimate the power of a well-chosen shoe or handbag! These seemingly subtle accessories are often the unsung heroes of professional attire. In this exciting adventure, Power Dressers, I'm equipping you with the tools to select shoes and purses that become powerful extensions of your rock star self. From the unwavering confidence that radiates from timeless pumps to the organized efficiency embodied in a structured tote bag, each stride and every item you carry will be a deliberate expression of your powerhouse persona. Join me, and let's step into a world where every shoe and handbag choice becomes a show-stopping statement of your brand.

> " Give a girl the right shoes, and she can conquer the world.
> – Marilyn Monroe "

  REFLECT ON YOUR ENVIRONMENT:
Consider the nature of your workplace and the specific dress code expectations. Reflect on the level of formality required in your industry. This will help guide your choices, and ensure your footwear and handbags align with the overall ambiance of your workplace.

2. ASSESS YOUR COMFORT NEEDS:
You should never compromise on comfort, especially when it comes to shoes and handbags you will be wearing for long hours. Consider your individual comfort preferences, such as heel height, cushioning, arch support, handbag weight, and handle or shoulder strap lengths. Prioritize designs that allow you to feel at ease, while exuding confidence.

3. EMBRACE VERSATILITY:
Invest in versatile footwear and handbags that seamlessly transition between various professional settings. Opt for neutral colors, like black, brown, or navy, that effortlessly complement a range of outfits. Versatility, such as classic pumps, loafers, ankle boots, and structured handbags, offer timeless appeal and maximize the usability of your accessories.

4. BALANCE WITH FUNCTIONALITY:
Strive for a harmonious balance of functionality in your footwear and handbag choices. Look for features like slip-resistant soles, ergonomic designs, and ample storage compartments in handbags. This ensures that your accessories look good and cater to your practical needs.

5. CONSIDER YOUR PERSONAL BRAND:
Evaluate the brand you wish to project through your footwear and handbags. If you aspire to convey a sense of dignified authority, opt for structured, sleek, and sophisticated designs. Alternatively, if you work in a creative industry, you might have more flexibility to experiment with unique pieces that infuse your personality into your brand.

6 PAY ATTENTION TO QUALITY AND CRAFTSMANSHIP:
Invest in well-crafted footwear and handbags made from high-quality materials. Quality shoes and handbags not only exude a sense of elegance, but also tend to be more durable, ensuring longevity and value for your investment. Prioritize brands known for their craftsmanship and attention to detail.

7 EXPERIMENT WITH TEXTURES AND PATTERNS:
Infuse your clothing toolbox with footwear and handbags featuring textures and patterns that add visual interest and personality. Consider options like textured leather, suede, or animal prints. These subtle details can subtly but boldly hit the right note.

8 CHOOSE APPROPRIATE HEEL HEIGHTS:
When selecting heel heights, consider your comfort level and work demands. Opt for manageable heel heights that allow you to navigate your workplace easily. Wedges or block heels can offer stability and support while maintaining a polished appearance.

9 SEEK EXPERT GUIDANCE:
If you need help with the proper footwear or handbag choices, consider seeking assistance from expert clothing and shoe stylists. They can provide personalized recommendations based on your preferences, body type, and workplace requirements.

10 CONSIDER HANDBAG SIZE AND FUNCTIONALITY:
Think about what you need from a handbag every day, in order to determine its size and usefulness. If you need room for a laptop, papers, or anything else, consider them

carefully. Select designs that provide various compartments and organizing features to maximize productivity and ensure your belongings will be secure.

I have compiled a few practical tips and suggestions to help you confidently select shoes and purses that complement your career goals and aspirations, while adding flair to your work attire. Your one-of-a-kind wardrobe can be crafted from an assortment of accessories by following these steps and thinking about how various styles, materials, and colors work together.

1. **OPT FOR CLASSIC PUMPS:**
    Invest in a pair of classic pumps with a moderate heel height in neutral colors like black or nude. Consider these shoes a cornerstone of your collection — they effortlessly complement everything from sleek tailored slacks to polished skirts. Their timeless design and endless styling possibilities make them true investment pieces. A comfortable, well-fitting pair can transform your posture and attitude.

2. **CONSIDER ANKLE BOOTS:**
    Ankle boots are a cold-weather staple for a reason! Not only do they keep your feet warm, but their stylish versatility can give an edge to your look. Whether you choose a sleek pointed-toe or a chunky-heeled style, a well-chosen pair of ankle boots adds a touch of both sophistication and individual flair to your outfit.

3. **CHOOSE STRUCTURED TOTE BAGS:**
    Invest in a well-crafted, structured tote bag made of high-quality materials like leather, canvas and Saffiano leather. Its clean lines and quality craftsmanship will showcase your organizational acumen and leadership preparation. Sturdy

construction ensures your essentials are protected, reflecting your meticulous approach to every aspect of your work.

4. **INCORPORATE SATCHEL BAGS:**
Satchel bags exude elegance and sophistication. Their design and functionality make them a good choice for those looking to project structure and reputable competence. Their spacious interior and multiple compartments provide ample space for documents, tech essentials, and other necessities for the modern professional.

5. **TRY A SLEEK CLUTCH:**
Nothing beats the understated elegance of a sleek clutch, which makes it perfect for formal events. Its streamlined shape and minimalist design effortlessly complement a polished day or evening look. The right clutch signifies your discerning taste, allowing your outfit and overall presence to shine.

6. **CONSIDER POINTED-TOE FLATS:**
Pointed-toe flats are a stylish solution for days when you need both comfort and polish. They embody the ideal compromise for workplace attire, offering the sleekness of heels without the discomfort. Consider them your secret weapon for tackling long commutes and busy workdays without sacrificing your sense of style.

7. **EXPERIMENT WITH STATEMENT HEELS:**
Slip into a pair of statement heels and unlock a bolder, more expressive version of yourself. Their sculpted design and eye-catching presence ignite your ensemble with a flash of personality. Embrace statement heels as a tool with

which to create a powerful aura and add a brushstroke of individuality.

8. **INCORPORATE VERSATILE BALLET FLATS:**
Ballet flats offer comfort and versatility while still maintaining a tasteful look. Inspired by the delicate footwear of dancers, they bring a touch of classic femininity to your stride. Whether embellished with a subtle bow or crafted from luxurious suede, ballet flats embody a timeless, graceful style.

9. **CONSIDER CROSSBODY BAGS:**
Embrace the practicality and chic appeal of a crossbody bag. Its adjustable strap and compact design offer effortless convenience, keeping your essentials close while allowing for freedom of movement as you navigate your day.

10. **EXPERIMENT WITH COLORFUL HANDBAGS:**
Incorporate colorful and vibrant handbags to add a pop of personality to your presentation. Add a touch of whimsy to your workwear with a playful, colorful handbag. Its unexpected pop of color can convey a cheerful energy and a hint of spontaneity. Consider it a subtle way to project your approachable personality and creative spirit.

Polishing Your Professional Image with Hair, Nails, Skincare, and Makeup

Your hair, nails, and makeup all contribute to your overall appearance. These parts of personal grooming are more than just aesthetic details; they are potent instruments that can boost your aura and radiate overall well-being. In this section, we'll look at how to refine your professional appearance with careful and purposeful hair, nail, skincare, and cosmetics selections.

> **Professional attire requires more than just choosing the right dress and accessories.**
> —Michele Grant

1. **PAY ATTENTION TO HAIR HEALTH:**
   Healthy, lustrous hair portrays a competent presence by radiating care and attention to refinement. Invest in quality hair care products and establish a hair-care routine that nourishes and protects your locks.

2. **INVEST IN A PROFESSIONAL HAIRSTYLE:**
   Your hairstyle speaks volumes about your dedication to presenting a polished image. Opt for a hairstyle that aligns with your personality and complements your face shape. Find a professional hairstylist who can guide you towards a high-quality hairstyle.

3. **OPT FOR CLASSIC, TIMELESS HAIRSTYLES:**
   Timeless hairstyles such as sleek bobs, buns, ponytails, or elegant chignons always stay in fashion, and exude sophistication. Classic hairstyles project intelligence and high caliber. Choose hairstyles that stay neat throughout the day and can transition from the office to after-work events with minimal effort.

4. MATCH YOUR HAIR COLOR TO YOUR SKIN TONE:

If you choose to dye your hair, consider shades that complement your skin tone. Matching your hair color to your skin tone can be helpful in highlighting your best features. A well-chosen hair color can also subtly soften the appearance of fine lines and wrinkles, creating a more youthful glow. Opt for a color that requires manageable upkeep and works well with your natural hair growth patterns to maintain a polished look.

5. PRACTICE NAIL CARE REGULARLY:

Healthy, well-maintained nails are a testament to your commitment to your personal brand and presentation. Make nail care a part of your self-care routine by moisturizing your cuticles, regularly buffing your nails, and trimming them to an appropriate length. Whether opting for a classic manicure or a minimalistic design, neat nails are a reflection of your thoroughness.

6. OPT FOR NEUTRAL NAIL COLORS:

When it comes to nail polish, neutral shades are timeless and classy. Colors like nude, pale pink, or light beige exude sophistication and complement a range of outfits. Their low-maintenance nature makes them perfect for busy professionals who want a polished look without frequent touch-ups. You can even try variations on these classics with a pearlescent finish, or a sheer wash of color for a contemporary touch.

7. APPLY HAND CREAM REGULARLY:

Keep your hands moisturized by applying hand cream throughout the day. Well-hydrated hands and nails portray a healthy and well-cared-for appearance. Choose a lightly scented lotion that complements your personal fragrance preferences. Also, try to select options with SPF to protect your skin from sun damage.

8. PRIORITIZE SKINCARE:
A well-maintained complexion exudes a sense of care and self-awareness. Establish a skincare routine that includes cleansing, moisturizing, and using sunscreen daily to protect your skin from environmental damage. Investing time in your skincare routine not only improves your appearance, but it is also an act of self-love that enhances your confidence and demonstrates a commitment to your long-term health and well-being.

9. WEAR SUNSCREEN DAILY:
Protecting your skin from harmful UV rays is necessary for maintaining a youthful and healthy appearance. Incorporate sunscreen with at least SPF 30 into your daily skincare routine, in order to shield your skin from premature aging and sun damage. Consistent sun protection is an essential step in preventing not only wrinkles but also serious skin health concerns. Make sunscreen a non-negotiable part of your routine — it's one of the easiest and most effective ways to invest in your skin health.

10. EXFOLIATE FOR A GLOWING COMPLEXION:
Discover the radiance beneath the surface! Regular exfoliation gently buffs away dull, tired skin cells, revealing a smoother and brighter complexion. By removing the build-up of dead skin cells, your serums and moisturizers can penetrate deeper for maximum effectiveness. Exfoliation is like prepping the canvas for your skincare masterpieces.

Think of it as a fresh start for your skin, enhancing its natural glow and revitalizing your overall appearance.

11 BE MINDFUL OF YOUR NECK AND DÉCOLLETAGE:
Your neck and décolletage are often overlooked, but they are important areas to care for, if you want to maintain a youthful appearance. Apply your skincare products, including sunscreen and moisturizer, to your neck and décolletage to keep these areas smooth and supple. Remember, consistent sun protection and hydration are vital for preventing wrinkles and crepey skin in these delicate areas.

12 EMPHASIZE YOUR EYES WITH MASCARA:
Define your lashes and enhance the natural beauty of your eyes with a swipe of mascara. It's a versatile essential that instantly adds polish and definition, perfect for both everyday wear and special occasions. Choose a mascara that adds volume and length without clumping.

13 MIND YOUR EYEBROWS:
Well-groomed eyebrows frame your face and can instantly elevate your appearance. Consider seeking skilled estheticians to help shape your eyebrows according to your face shape and preference. A well-defined brow can add a touch of elegance to your overall look.

14 CHOOSE A FLATTERING LIP COLOR:
Lipstick can be a powerful tool in projecting assurance and authority. Select a lip color that complements your skin tone and brightens your face. Depending on your business culture, go for a bold red or a vibrant berry shade that can instantly transform your energy, signaling confidence and

a willingness to take charge. Express your unique style by experimenting with different shades and textures — from a classic satin finish to a trendy matte liquid lipstick.

15 HIGHLIGHT YOUR LIPS WITH LIP LINER:
Using lip liners can enhance the shape and definition of your lips, creating a more polished and refined appearance. Invest in a lip liner that matches your lip color or leans a smidgen darker in hue, to prevent feathering and ensure a long-lasting finish.

Adopting and regularly practicing these techniques will help you enhance your powerhouse aesthetic through your hair, nails, skin, and cosmetics. Maintaining a well-groomed appearance is an art form that will help you to stand out from the crowd. To boost your self-assurance, skillfully accessorize with jewelry and accessories, choose distinctive shoes and purses, and perfect your grooming routine.

• • •

Chapter 8 will take us on an adventure into the excitement of maintaining a professional wardrobe that is up-do-date. Now is the moment to tackle the ever-changing world of trends, effortlessly solidifying your relevance and presence.

Power Dressers, let's jump right in and keep making your experience extraordinary.

chapter 8

STAYING FASHION-FORWARD IN YOUR PROFESSIONAL LIFE

French fashion designer Yves Saint Laurent once said, "Fashion fades, style is eternal." It's a delicate dance for the Power Dresser, who strives to be in the vanguard of fashion without losing the timelessness of distinguished style. This chapter is a guide to this intricate ballet, which aims to help you express your fashion-forward self while staying true to your brand.

Here are the topics we'll cover:

- **Understanding the role of trends in professional style**
- **Pairing trendy and classic pieces for a fashion-forward look**
- **Staying current with industry trends and norms**

Don't shy away from experimenting with bolder trends within your power wardrobe. Power dressing in the modern world demands a nuanced approach. While polished tailoring and classic silhouettes remain cornerstones, strategically incorporating fashion-forward elements positions you as a forward-thinking leader who isn't afraid to challenge convention while maintaining an air of professionalism. This demonstrates an agile mindset and a willingness to evolve — qualities that command respect in any professional setting.

Understanding the Role of Trends in Professional Style

> "Fashion," Donatella Versace once observed, "is about dreaming and making other people dream."

At the core of power dressing, there's a need to incorporate the ebbs and flows of fashion trends, to help your image evolve and convey a sense of dynamism.

At first sight, people may believe that trends have little to do with the world of Power Dressers.

In fact, they play an *important role*. *Understanding* and *adopting trends* demonstrates that you are in sync with the *times*, while also signaling your *versatility* and *forward-thinking perspective*, which are highly valued in today's fast-changing *corporate scene*.

But how can you remain steadfast in your first-rate business look while keeping your finger on the pulse of fashion? Using these practical tips, you'll be able to navigate the maze of current fashion trends, and pick and choose which ones to incorporate into your work wardrobe.

1. **UNDERSTAND THE TREND:**
    The first step is understanding the trend — what it represents, its origins, and its significance. A trend isn't just about a new color, pattern, or fad. It symbolizes societal transformations in preferences and perspectives. For instance, the emergence of power dressing during the 1980s correlated with a surge in women stepping into the workplace and asserting their influence.

2. **EVALUATE ITS RELEVANCE:**
    Not all trends will align with your brand and career aspirations, or the industry you're in. You'll need to evaluate each trend's relevance to your environment context. Is it something you can incorporate into your workwear? Is it a trend that would resonate with your industry's norms? To help with this, try following industry-specific media channels and attending industry events; these will be an effective method for discerning relevant trends.

3. **ADOPT IN MODERATION:**
    When incorporating trends, moderation is key. As Ralph Lauren said, "Fashion is not necessarily about labels. It's not about brands. It's about something else that comes from within you." A trendy blouse or a fashionable accessory can make your outfit current, but your overall look should still echo the sophisticated tone of a Power Dresser.

EXPERIMENT AND EVOLVE:
Don't be afraid to experiment. Fashion is a creative field, and there's always room for personal interpretation. Try different ways to incorporate a trend into your outfits, and don't be disheartened if it doesn't work out the first time. Remember, it's all about finding what works best for you.

I remember when color-blocking was a trend, a few years ago. It was everywhere — from the runways to the street-style stars. While the more adventurous fashionistas were mixing bold and contrasting colors, I had to find a way to make it work for the corporate environment. My solution was to pair neutrals like beige and white with a single bright color, like cobalt blue or Kelly green with a contrasting complementary color handbag, cardigan, or accessory like a beret. This approach allowed me to take advantage of the trend without sacrificing the distinguished deportment required in my workspace.

SEEK INSPIRATION:
Look to fashion-forward leaders in your industry for inspiration. They may have already done some of the legwork in figuring out which trends work within your specific practice. Use social media, industry publications, and real-life interactions to glean ideas and insights.

> **Style is a way to say who you are without having to speak.**
> –Rachel Zoe

A few years ago, the fashion industry saw a revival of the oversized silhouettes of the 80s. As a senior executive in a tech firm, adopting this trend presented a challenge on my frame. My solution was a hybrid approach. I opted for a slightly oversized navy blazer, balanced with fitted trousers. This balance of proportions struck the right note between trendy and traditional. It sparked intriguing conversations among my colleagues and affirmed my position as an empowering and innovative Power Dresser, illustrating that even bold trends can find a place in the corporate world, with a bit of creative styling.

As we delve deeper into this chapter, remember that trends are not a mandate but an invitation to explore and evolve your story. As you keep your style up to date, keep it undeniably *you* — a testament to your unique journey and story of becoming your best self.

Appreciating trends and their place in a Power Dresser's wardrobe isn't just about being fashionable. It's about being in tune with the times, expressing your creativity, and demonstrating your adaptability — all of which can make powerful statements and bring positive energy.

Pairing Trendy and Classic Pieces for a Fashion-Forward Look

Now that we have a handle on how to understand trends, let's delve into the actual process of incorporating these on-trend pieces into your professional wardrobe.

1. **FIND THE HARMONY BETWEEN MODERN AND CLASSIC:**
   Navigating the tightrope between classic sophistication and modern savvy is crucial. Reflect on the time when oversized

belts were the fashion craze. Instead of adopting the most dramatic version, which would have compromised my elegant appearance, I opted for a moderately wide belt in a subdued color. It was the perfect compromise; it was trendy, yet it did not detract from the crisp brilliance my attire exuded.

I adhere to the sage advice of Coco Chanel, who said, "Before you leave the house, look in the mirror and take one thing off." This principle is especially beneficial when implementing trends into your outfit — it implies the application of a hint of modernity instead of a complete trend overhaul.

2 CREATE A DIALOGUE BETWEEN PIECES:

Aim for a dialogue between your outfit's classic and current pieces. One element should complement and enhance the others, resulting in a coherent look. Your style narrative should demonstrate your ability to expertly combine ephemeral and timeless pieces into a compelling, unified statement.

3 IMPLEMENT THE RULE OF THIRDS:

When blending the trendy and the classic, consider following the rule of thirds, a concept borrowed from the world of visual art. This principle suggests that an outfit divided into thirds is more pleasing to the eye. Translate this to your outfit by incorporating two parts classic, one part trendy, or vice versa, depending on your comfort level.

4 CREATE FOCAL POINTS:

One way to effortlessly incorporate trendy pieces is to create a focal point with one trendy piece. This item should attract immediate attention and set the tone for the rest of your outfit. It could be a pair of uniquely cut trousers, a bold handbag, or a statement necklace. Once you've established this, build the rest of your outfit with classic pieces that complement your focal point.

I remember when geometric patterns were trending heavily. I saw an opportunity to leverage this trend by purchasing a silk scarf with a striking geometric print. I would pair this scarf with a classic white button-down shirt and black tailored trousers. The classic pieces complemented the scarf, without competing for the spotlight.

5. **RE-IMAGINE LAYERING:**
A trend that has been around for a few years now is layering a turtleneck under a dress. I've paired lightweight, sleek turtlenecks, silk blouses, and even collar bibs under classic shift dresses, for an extra touch of sophistication and versatility. These combinations added a layer of visual interest, while preserving the professionalism of the outfit.

6. **INCORPORATE PANTONE'S COLOR OF THE YEAR:**
Annually, Pantone announces its Color of the Year, which frequently sets the tone in the fashion industry. Imbibe this color into your clothing collection. For instance, if "Very Peri" is the Pantone Color of the Year, consider integrating it through a chic blouse or an elegant skirt, to keep your ensemble trendy and lively.

As you apply these techniques, recall the timeless wisdom of Coco Chanel: "Fashion fades, only style remains the same." Welcome trends, but don't overlook your timeless signature brand.

7   GET EDGY WITH SUITING:
When deconstructed or mismatched suiting becomes a fashion trend, there's no need to hesitate. By merging a classic blazer with a modern asymmetric skirt, or trousers with a bold stripe, you create a stylish fusion that nods to the trend but remains grounded in professionalism. Maintain a balanced aesthetic by keeping the rest of your outfit and accessories subtle. Pair the look with a simple, sophisticated blouse and understated jewelry. This allows the focus to stay on the fashion-forward suiting, giving you an edge without losing your classy vibe.

8   COLOR-BLOCK WITH TRENDY HUES:
Bold, vibrant colors can be daunting, but when they're in trend, they offer an exciting way to refresh your Power Dresser wardrobe. The color-blocking technique can be your ally here. Pair a blouse or skirt in a trendy color with a timeless neutral piece. For example, if "Radiant Orchid" is the color du jour, harmonize an orchid-hued blouse with a classic black pencil skirt. Complement the look with navy blue shoes, a handbag and minimal silver or gold jewelry pieces to allow the color-block effect to shine. The result will be a striking ensemble that puts you ahead of the fashion curve.

9   USE INNOVATIVE OUTERWEAR:
Outerwear often serves as a canvas for fashion trends, be it long line blazers or oversized trench coats. Leverage this by overlaying these trendy pieces over monochromatic classic outfits. A neutral, monochrome base makes the trendy contemporary outerwear stand out, creating a visually striking yet sophisticated look. Opt for outfits in colors such as black, white, or navy to ensure the outerwear piece is the

star of the show. This blend of classic and contemporary signals your awareness of current fashion trends, without sacrificing your smart, elegant demeanor.

10. **SKILLFULLY INTEGRATE STREET-STYLE TRENDS:**
Street-style trends are known for their boldness and creativity, but you needn't discard them as being too daring for the professional sphere. Instead, weave these trends with a light hand into your work attire. Select an accessory or a singular piece of clothing that epitomizes the trend and combine it with your more traditional attire.

Consider the period when neon made a comeback in the street-style scene, splashing city streets with vibrant hues. While neon colors might seem a tad too flashy for the corporate world, I found a way to embrace the trend in a creative manner. I chose a lime green silk scarf, a relatively small but potent accessory, and teamed it with a charcoal gray slim fit pantsuit and lime green open toe kitten heels.

The neon scarf and dainty kitten heels not only added an unexpected pop of color to the ensemble but also injected a dose of fun into an otherwise staid outfit. The trick here is to let your imagination have a bit of fun, resulting in a surprise that sparks conversations and positive energy.

Staying Current with Industry Trends and Norms

*"**The ever-changing world of business is always** keeping us on our toes, and the fashion trends that go along with it are no exception.*

—**Michele Grant**

Staying abreast of these shifts offers you a subtle but impactful advantage. Skillfully blend current trends with the timeless expectations of your field to elevate your professional image, showcasing your contemporary perspective. This delicate balance demonstrates a nuanced understanding of the workplace, allowing you to project a modern, sophisticated presence that sets you apart.

Here's a step-by-step guide to stay on top of industry trends and norms:

1. **KNOW YOUR INDUSTRY'S CULTURE:**
   Every industry has its own uniform, so to speak. Finance has a different dress code to tech, and the creative fields differ vastly from academia. Spend time observing the fashion choices of colleagues and industry leaders. Notice how they incorporate current trends into their wardrobe.

2. **ATTEND INDUSTRY EVENTS:**
   These are great places to see the latest trends in your field in action, from conferences to casual meetups. Observe what successful people in your industry wear and note how it differs from general fashion trends.

3. **FOLLOW RELEVANT INFLUENCERS:**
   There are influencers who are known for their style in every field. Follow them on social media to gain insights into the latest trends. Look out for elements they build into their dressing and how they balance fashion-forward and industry-appropriate.

4. **READ INDUSTRY-SPECIFIC MAGAZINES:**
   Publications like *Forbes*, *Business Insider*, and *Adweek* often feature industry leaders, and provide glimpses

into their wardrobe choices. These insights can serve as a guide to dressing for your particular industry while staying fashionable.

5. CONSTANTLY REFRESH YOUR WARDROBE:
You don't need to overhaul your wardrobe with each new trend. But adding a few on-trend pieces each season can keep your wardrobe up-to-date and relevant. Remember, the goal is to subtly incorporate trends, not to become a fashion victim.

6. USE TECH TOOLS TO STAY INFORMED:
Consider leveraging digital platforms such as Pinterest or Instagram to identify emerging fashion trends. Tools like these provide visual representations of popular trends and can give you a sense of how to incorporate them into your work wardrobe.

7. ANALYZE YOUR COMPANY'S BRAND COLORS:
Many companies and industries have specific color palettes associated with them. By subtly incorporating these colors into your outfit, you can create a visual alignment with your company's brand, displaying an additional layer of innovation and influence.

8. USE A STYLE DIARY:
Track your outfits, the relationships you initiated when wearing them, and the reactions they elicit over time. This record-keeping could provide valuable insights into what works best in your industry environment. It's a unique, personalized way of studying the impact of your wardrobe choices.

9. **LEVERAGE STYLE APPS:**
Use apps like LTK (LIKEtoKNOW.it), Style DNA, and 21 Buttons to try out new trends without committing to buying. They also offer personalized recommendations that could help you discover new ways of blending your attire with current trends.

10. **UTILIZE VIRTUAL FITTING ROOMS:**
Technological advances have made it possible to virtually try on clothes before purchasing them. Platforms like ASOS, for example, offer this technology. It allows you to explore a wide range of options, helping you stay up to date with fashion trends without breaking the bank or wasting time on returns.

11. **TAKE NOTE OF INDUSTRY LEADERS:**
Who are the industry leaders or high-profile individuals in your field? Take note of how they present themselves. The idea is not to copy their style, but you can certainly take cues from them. They're probably on top of industry norms, and their wardrobe choices might inspire your own.

12. **START A STYLE INSPIRATION BOARD:**
Use a platform like Pinterest to start a board dedicated to professional style inspiration. You can add photos from various sources that reflect the current industry trends and norms, which you can refer to whenever you need some motivation.

13. **HIRE A PERSONAL SHOPPER OR STYLIST:**
While this may sound extravagant, many department stores offer complimentary personal shopper services. The

associates are trained to know current trends and how they can adapt these as a canvas to different profiles.

14. **ATTEND VIRTUAL FASHION SHOWS:**
Fashion weeks around the world are now offering virtual attendance. Watching these shows provides insights into upcoming trends, and you can adapt these to your dynamic clothing toolbox.

15. **DOWNLOAD FASHION-FOCUSED APPS:**
Apps like Smart Closet and Shoplook help you rediscover hidden gems in your wardrobe and plan effortless workweek outfits. Visualize how different pieces work together, find the perfect trend-aligned additions, and even create capsule wardrobes for specific professional settings. But the options don't stop there! Explore the world of fashion organization and outfit planning apps to find the perfect digital stylist for your unique needs.

> You can't just be. You
> have to be who you are.
> —Michele Grant

You are not dressing merely to impress but to express a harmonious blend of your unique personal style and a clear understanding of your industry's culture.

Keep an *open mind*, keep *learning*, and remember to have *fun with fashion*!

The wisdom you've gleaned from this chapter will transform the maze of trendy fashion into an intelligible map. It's a terrain that provides a space to build opportunities to continuously spotlight one's ingenuity, vibrancy, and dynamism that's inherent in the rhythm of change.

• • •

As we took the winding path through this chapter, we learned that integrating fashion-forward trends into our business wardrobe reflects more than just Power Dresser savvy; it's also a testament to our innovative essence, and the driving force behind every trailblazer. Fashion trends may ebb and flow, but your style should remain an eternal echo of your brand. That's the true power of a Power Dresser.

the grand finale

FROM STYLE NOVICES TO POWER DRESSERS

Power Dressers, the final pages are upon us, but your journey is just beginning to flourish. From understanding your body type to navigating complex dress codes and infusing your individuality into your style, each chapter of this book was a steppingstone to your ultimate transformation. This metamorphosis from the cocoon of uncertainties to the vibrant butterfly of a Power Dresser is your personal tale of triumph.

We've journeyed together through the pages of this book exploring the myriad ways power dressing can elevate your career, boost your confidence, and help you to make a statement. The road to becoming a Power Dresser is not a one-way path; it's a continuous journey, much like the fashion industry itself. As this initial part of the journey draws to a close, it is an opportune moment to step back and appreciate how much ground we have covered. From understanding body types and the psychology of colors to incorporating sustainable fashion and navigating complex dress codes, you have armed yourself with knowledge. Moreover, as we all would agree, knowledge is power.

A Power Dresser's journey is an exhilarating voyage of self-expression, empowerment, and continuous evolution. As you close this book, it's not the end but the exciting onset of a new chapter in your life.

As we traversed the plethora of key principles and invaluable tools in this guide, a fundamental truth emerged: the transformative power of style is a reflection of the transformative power within you. Every chapter, sentence, and word had an intrinsic purpose: to help you embrace *your* unique style. A style that projects authority cultivates respect and, most importantly, fosters self-confidence.

As the esteemed, multi-award-winning actress Viola Davis so powerfully states, *"You can't be hesitant about who you are."* These words encapsulate the essence of the Power Dresser's journey. Through this *exploration*, you're learning not just discovering the *nuances* of *fabrics*, *cuts*, and *colors* but delving into the depths of your own *uniqueness* and *identity*.

Let's take a moment to revel in your evolution.

The essence of being a Power Dresser is knowing how to highlight your strengths, physically and mentally. Chapter 2 equipped you with this critical understanding, enhancing your self-perception and, consequently, other people's perceptions.

In Chapter 3, Color psychology unfolded another dimension of power dressing. By strategically choosing colors that radiate authority, confidence, and ambition, you have a unique edge with which to influence those around you positively.

Remember Chapter 4? We ventured into the terrain of sustainability, not just as a trend, but as a lifestyle, empowering you to make eco-conscious and ethical choices that reflect your values.

As we untangled the web of dress codes in Chapter 5, it was about more than just rules. It was about adapting and making strategic choices that exude your powerhouse brand with finesse.

Chapter 6 presented an exciting vista where we explored attire's nonverbal and cultural language. You're not just dressing for your job, but also to communicate your intent, your respect for diversity, and your adaptability.

Chapter 7 accentuated your style journey by highlighting the crucial details of accessories, footwear, and grooming. These seemingly small elements can magnify your confidence and refine your persona.

Lastly, in Chapter 8, we acknowledged the whimsical nature of trends and the fun they can bring to our wardrobes. Staying current is not just about being fashionable; it also signifies your openness to change, innovative spirit, and dynamic personality.

Power Dressers, you are now well-equipped to step out into the world, armed with the knowledge and skills to make choices that empower and inspire. However, remember that true style is a journey, not a destination. It evolves as you grow in your career and personal life. It is my hope that this guide serves as a trusted companion on your journey, providing valuable insights and advice when you need them.

> "*Fashion is ephemeral.*
> *It is the flavor of the day.*
> *Style is forever.*
> *It is a classic work of art.*"
> **—Michele Grant**

You've reached a new apex so don't just follow fashion but make it your own, crafting a distinct identity that is timeless and invincible.

At its core, fashion is an authentic expression of self, an affirmation of identity. As the iconic model and businesswoman Tyra Banks said, "Never dull your shine for somebody else." And that's the mantra you should carry forward from this book — always maintain your unique style for everyone and everything.

Your transformation will be immense and will undoubtedly reverberate in all aspects of your life. The Power Dresser in you is not just about outward appearances, but also a reflection of your inner strength, wisdom, and individuality.

Coco Chanel once advised, *"Always keep your head, heels, and standards high,"* Let this be your guiding light in your journey as a Power Dresser (perhaps with the exception of the high heels). Have **high standards** for *yourself*, your *style*, and your *aspirations*.

The exhilarating experiences that lie ahead are full of endless possibilities. You have the knowledge, the tools, and the confidence to face them head-on. Power Dressers, you're set to revolutionize the world, one outfit at a time and I cannot wait to see how your professional style evolves as you continue to shine, inspire, and conquer. Remember, your style is a testament to your strength. Own it; flaunt it; live it!

People who have incredible style and individuality are the ones who live life to the fullest. So, why not jump right in and enjoy this exciting adventure? It's time for you to take on the world.

Go live your best life, Power Dressers!

Join The Power Dressers community at **www.powerdressers.com** for style tips, expert advice, and inspiration.

Media Inquiries & Speaking Engagements: **outreach@powerdressers.com**

www.ingramcontent.com/pod-product-compliance
Lightning Source LLC
Chambersburg PA
CBHW051944290426
44110CB00015B/2100